AF553465

SELF-HELP GROUPS AND WOMEN EMPOWERMENT

SELF-HELP GROUPS AND WOMEN EMPOWERMENT

Dr. K.R. MURUGAN
Associate Professor & Head I/C
Department of Women's Studies
Alagappa University
Karaikudi (Tamil Nadu)

REGAL PUBLICATIONS
New Delhi - 110 027

SELF-HELP GROUPS AND WOMEN EMPOWERMENT

ISBN 978-81-8484-372-9

Typeset by
THE LASER PRINTERS
8/15, 3rd Floor, Subhash Nagar, New Delhi-110027

Printed in India at
MAYUR ENTERPRISES,
WZ Plot No. 3, Gujjar Market, Tihar Village, New Delhi-110018

Published by
REGAL PUBLICATIONS
F-159, Rajouri Garden, New Delhi-110027
Phones: 45546396, 25435369
E-mail: regalbookspub@yahoo.com, regaldeepbooks@yahoo.com

Contents

Preface

Women empowerment and gender equality has been recognized as the important components of Millennium Development Goals. Empowerment is the process of building capacities of creating an atmosphere which enables people to fully realize their creative potential in pursuance of quality of life. It is an active, multidimensional process which enables women to realize their full identity and powers in all spheres of life.

Women constitute 49% of the total population of India as per Census and constituting half of the population, are the most important human resources central to development of any race, culture and civilization. But the condition of women when we see through the prism of gender equality and gender parity looks terribly miserable. In all walks of life women are lagging behind. The representations of women are less in prominent fields and remain a marginal force in polities, industry and administration. Hence the National Mission for Empowerment of Women was launched by Government of India in 2010 to strengthen overall programmes that promote all round development of women. This will achieve gender equality and gender justice and holistic development of women through inter-sectoral convergence of programme relating to women, forging synergy between various stakeholders and creating an enabling environment conducive to social change.

Self-help groups are proved to be very fruitful not only for the empowerment of women but also for the holistic community development. The role of Self-help groups are vital to implement all the development programme to fulfill the real objectives. Self-help groups act as the agents of empowering women. Empowerment is long-term process of social transformation, which changes the expiring particular system and strengthens the form of marginalized women who have no social awareness, economic independence and security. Thus self-help group serves as a mean to empower women. This book will contribute to understand the abstract of women empowerment and self-help group which is the vital component for sustainable development.

Dr. K.R. MURUGAN

Self-Help Group: Concept, Nature and Functions

- Introduction
- Self-Help as Methodology
- Self-Help Group: International Scenario
- BACC System in Thailand
- Grameen Bank in Bangladesh
- Self-Help Group: National Scenario
- Government Programmes and Self-Help Groups
- Self-Help Groups in Tamil Nadu
- Self-Help Groups: Boon to Holistic Development

INTRODUCTION

Globally gender equality and women empowerment has been recognized as the important components of millennium development goal. For the empowerment of women at gross root level Self-Help Group has emerged as the most vital instrument in the process of participatory approach. Self-help group is a media to achieve the objective of rural development and to get community participation in all rural development programmes. The government and non-government organizations promote a formation of self-help groups and utilize services of several group as the agents of women development projects and rural development. However, organizing small and cohesive group of women with defined goals to attain is a fundamental requirement for any empowerment process. Realizing this the government along with non-governmental organizations started to organize small and cohesive group of women. These groups later came to be known as women's Self-Help Groups. Self-Help Groups plays a very prominent role in the social transformation of women and has emerged as a new appropriate force for removing poverty.

Self-Help Groups begin with savings and credit activities, later they engage in productive economic and social activities, but also functions as important sustainable, democratic and women managed institutions. The saving habit is an instrumental in an initiation and of knowledge about health, nutrition, literacy, women's rights, childcare, education, adoption of new agricultural practices, farms and non-farm sector economic activities, etc. and paved the way for increased participation of women in decision-making in households, community and the local democratic set-up besides helping to prepare women to leadership position. The rural women are the marginalized groups in the society because of socio-economic competition. They remain backward and in the lower position of the social ladder. They can lift themselves from the poverty and stagnation through micro-finance and formation of Self-Help Groups.

Self-Help Groups approach is the key element of social mobilization being devoid of and politicization. It provides credit to rural women on easy turns with access to several income-generating activities. SHG is an organized forum to disburse micro-credit to the rural women for the purpose of making them enterprising women and encouraging them to enter into entrepreneurial activities. SHG caters the credit needs of the rural women. SHG has an autonomous structure at the level and through their regular meetings and their collections, they are expected not only to inculcate a habit of saving amongst their members, but also have a group solid as well as a feeling of mutual and concern. The self-help groups being composite units at levels consist in their members a sense of responsibility.

A group of women formed together as social group to achieve certain objectives for themselves and for the society is referred as Self-Help Groups. Women are motivated to form into groups by Government and Non-Governmental Organizations and are entertained the savings habit. They are trained to open bank account and save amount regularly. The office-bearers of the group assist the members to maintain group savings, which would be later, utilized as seed money to receive further loans from banks for income generating activities. The activity of the self-help group started with group savings, which enable them to enhance their social, economic, and political power.

Self-Help Groups create awareness and provide self-confidence among the members. Further SHG provides an atmosphere to develop inter-caste relations. Groups help women to communicate freely with one another. This leads to decision-making capacity at home and at work. Self-Help Groups are small homogeneous, voluntary groups of by rural poor formed to cultivate the habit of savings from their earnings to the common fund and provide internal audit service. In the members for matching their production and emergent consumption needs. It is a democratic institution and it is transparency. SHG is a form of solidarity, harmony and to make the rural women socially empowered, economically self-reliant and politically participatory and involve them in the mainstream of community development.

SELF-HELP AS METHODOLOGY

The concept of self-help has a history in the women's movement, in particular, the women's health movement. In self-help processes one naturally begins with the self; All the participants share their own experiences of conflicts and struggles, strengths and weaknesses and help each other identify individual and collective strategies for empowerment. This sharing gives the participants a new sense of individual and collective strength, helps foster trust and respect for the diversity in the group and strengthens their ability to constructively question and critique. To enable such a process to really take place, it is crucial that the facilitation create spaces which are democratic, free from prejudices, non-judgmental, non-competitive and non-hierarchical.

In the context of health, the members of the Boston Women's Health collective in the United States of America first used self-help methodology to explore and gain control over their bodies. This process challenged norms of shame, privacy and pollution associated with women's bodies the world over, as well as the hierarchy between medical, professionals and women. The self-help has been co-opted by aid agencies, governments, credit co-operatives and multinationals and is being used to further economic growth is being recommended. The objectives of the training were to:

- Assist women to recast their self-image and confidence by acknowledging their potentials, validating their experiences and knowledge, and improving their health through self-help skills.
- Uncover and probe into gender-class and caste-based biases and trends in the medical system and in society, and demystify the myths created around our bodies.
- Look into and challenge beliefs, practices and institutions through which men control and exploit women's minds, emotions, labour, sexuality, fertility and property.
- Encourage individual and collective action and networking for women's empowerment.
- Look at health as a basic right and press for Government and social accountability to the concerns of women.
- Evolve a socialist feminist perspective on women's health and healing systems. [Ranjani K. Murthy, 2001].

SELF-HELP GROUP: INTERNATIONAL SCENARIO

The Self-Help Group concept is a silent revolution taking place in the rural credit system in many parts of the world.

BAAC System in Thailand

The BAAC (Bank for Agriculture and Agricultural Co-operatives) was set-up in 1966 for direct loans to farmers as well as to co-operatives in Thailand. By 1974, the BAAC opened branches in 58 out of 71 provinces. Thailand's economy is basically dependent of agricultural with about 76 per cent of its population engaged in farming. From 1916 onwards, Thailand has been experimenting with various institutional frameworks for providing cheap credit to the rural sector. Farmers were engaged to set-up co-operatives for easy access to loans from government agencies through the co-operative structure.

The rural credit system in Thailand comprises commercial

banks, the BAAC, and Cooperative institutions both at the apex and intermediate levels. Farmers' cooperatives are organised under the names of 'agricultural cooperative societies' and 'farmer associations', etc. Thrust is now being placed on the formation and development of autonomous informal Self-Help Groups (SHG). The BAAC plays an importance role in dispersing rural credit and undertaking various operations that connected with such credit extension.

The BAAC provides financial services to about half the farmer households in Thailand and is a state owned enterprise. The BAAC's objectives are to promote occupation of farmers to ensure adequate incomes to raise their living standards and to develop agriculture as a key factor in the national economy. The BAAC operates through 118 branches spread all over the country and 604 field offices. The BAAC also functions of an agent of government in undertaking various activities like building linkages, provision of infrastructural support, procurement of food grains, etc. The BAAC lends directly to individual farmers and farmers' institutions comprise agricultural occupations. Farmers' institutions comprise agricultural cooperatives and registered farmers' associations. The credits extended by the BAAC to individual farmers one in both cash and kind. Agricultural co-operatives and registered farmers' associations enable the farmers to hold equity in their organization and attempt to improve the living standards of their members.

Types of loans extended by the BAAC were mainly short-term loans for purchasing form supplies and agricultural machinery, for purchasing and marketing of agricultural products, loans against pledge of farm produce, etc. medium and long-term loans were for investment in agricultural fixed assets. Long-term loans for refinancing of old debts or for land redemption were also made available to individual farmers. It also gives loans for construction of houses. The BAAC is currently concentrating or lending through autonomous informed groups. This is still in the pilot stage. There are more than 8,900 Self-Help Groups with a membership of 5,74,000 in Thailand and many of them issue loans for agriculture and other productive activities (K.G. Karmaker, 2005).

Grameen Bank in Bangladesh

Grameen Bank (GB) has reversed conventional banking practice by removing the need for collateral and a banking system based on mutual trust, accountability, participation and creativity. GB provides credit to the poorest of the poor in rural Bangladesh, without any collateral. At GB, credit is a cost effective weapon to fight poverty and it serves as a catalyst in the overall development of socio-economic conditions of the poor who have been kept outside the banking orbit on the ground that they are poor and hence not bankable. Professor Muhammad Yunus, the founder of "Grameen Bank" and its Managing Director, reasoned that if financial resources can be made available to the poor people on terms and conditions that are appropriate and reasonable, "these millions of small people with their millions of small pursuits can add up to create the biggest development wonder."

As of May, 2006, it has 6.67 million borrowers, 97 percent of whom are women. With 2247 branches, GB provides services in 72,096 villages, covering more that 86 percent of the total villages in Bangladesh.

Grameen Bank's positive impact on its poor and formerly poor borrowers has been documented in many independent studies carried out by external agencies including the World Bank, the International Food Research Policy Institute (IFPRI) and the Bangladesh Institute of Development Studies (BIDS).

The Grameen Bank owes its origin to the concern felt by its founder, Dr. Muhammad Yunus at the pitiable condition of landless women labourers, who were exploited both by their masters and in their own families. Dr. Yunus felt that if these women could work for themselves instead of working for others, they could retain much of the surplus generated by their labour, currently appropriated by others and benefit their families. Other reasons for selecting rural women especially, as the target beneficiaries, were to elevate their social status within their own families so as to reduce male domination in introduction bound and conservative society and the conviction that women folk, as more responsible family leaders, were quick and sincere enough to seize opportunities for improving the economic conditions of their families. The missing ingredient was credit. Funds were required to improve their economic conditions through self-employment without government or external assistance or subsidies. The guiding concept was that the poor know best how to improve their economic conditions provided adequate credit was made available. The translation of this simple idea into practice gave birth to an imaginative project, which has grown to attract worldwide appreciations. The initial scheme was started as a village credit society in December 1976 in Jobra, a village adjacent to Chittagong University, where Dr. Junus was of teacher in economics. At first, credit arrangements were made with one of the nearby banks and the economic programme of the Chittagong University under the leadership of Dr. Yunus. The success of the experiment evoked interest among more banks. In June 1979, the Central Bank of the Country, the Bangladesh Bank stepped in and organised sponsorship from several nationalized commercial banks for extension of the scheme to more areas. In 1980, the project caught international attention and financial aid started flowing in from different donor institutions like IFAD, Ford Foundation, NORAD, SIDA, GTZ, etc.

One of the strong points of the Grameen Bank is the extraordinary commitment and dedication of its field staff and all one thoroughly rural-oriented. The lending policies of the Grameen Bank are totally revolutionary and deviate in many aspects from the traditional approach. Foremost among these is the principle that 'the bank will go to the client; the client will not come to the bank'. In other words, the bank earmarked certain groups viz. landless and assetless, as its target borrowers and anyone belonging to the target group could approach and obtain credit assistance. Even within the target group, the bank focuses its attentions on women. As on 1992, out of the twelve lakh members of the bank 93% were women members.

Credit assistance was supported by other social measures to bring about self-reliance, discipline, awareness of obligations to society and even physical fitness and health care, amongst its borrowers. The compulsory savings element and the purposes for which it would be put to use, have taught the members about the importance and benefits of thrift and mutual help. Lending is not security-oriented purely reliance in placed on people.

Grameen Bank has established priorities for membership enrolment within the target population. The priority targets are:

- Single female heads of households (widow, deserted divorce),
- Persons from household not owning any land, and
- persons owning is homestead but no other hand.

Other criteria are:

- number of dependent children, and
- Occurs to other sources of support.

Grameen Bank—Group Formation

Instead of individual, group basis was entertained for loan proposals. Each group should have atleast five members. The first member will be identified by the bank staff and thereafter, the member is expected in get four other like minded members. Six such groups federate into a centre and each center has a common meeting place on a definite day and time of the week. No members can belong to more than one group and members of a group cannot be blood relation. Members of a group should also belong to the same village and should not be indebted to any other credit institution.

For the first seven days, meetings of the group are required to be held every day, when the obligations of the borrowers are explained. Each member of the group is also required to save one taka a day and at the end of week, takas 35 should be deposited by the group with the branch. Each group also elects a chairman and secretary during the period. Thereafter, the group is recognized. The responsibilities of the group chairman consist of convening meetings, collecting recoveries and contributing to various funds, recommending of loan proposals.

The Grameen Bank's activities attach considerable importance to self-reliance and savings. Apart from savings each member also has to contribute to two other funds. There are Centre Emergency Fund and Children's Welfare Fund which are maintained at the centres. These funds are utilized for supplementary assistance to the group members.

The essence of the Grameen Bank project is social development; credit is used as a catalyst in the process. All members of the Grameen Bank have agreed upon certain obligations called the "16 decisions".

1. The four principles of Grameen Bank—discipline, unity, courage and hard work—we shall follow and advance in all walks of our lives.
2. We shall bring prosperity to our families.
3. We shall not lie in dilapidated houses. We shall repair our houses and work towards constructing new houses as soon as possible.

4. We shall grow vegetables all the year round. We shall eat plenty of them and sell the surplus.
5. During the planting season, we shall plant as many seedlings as possible.
6. We shall plan to keep our families small. We shall minimise our expenditure. We shall look after our health.
7. We shall educate our children and ensure that they can earn enough to pay for their education.
8. We shall keep our children and the environment clean.
9. We shall build and use pit latrines.
10. We shall drink tube-well water, if it is not available, we shall boil water or use alum.
11. We shall not take any dowry in our sons' weddings neither shall we give any dowry in our daughters' weddings. We shall keep the centre free from the curse of dowry. We shall not practice child marriage.
12. We shall not inflict any injustice on anyone, neither shall we allow anyone to do so.
13. For higher income, we shall collectively undertake bigger investments.
14. We shall always be ready to help each other. If anyone is in difficulty, we shall all help.
15. If we come to know of any breach of discipline in any centre, we shall all go there and restore discipline.
16. We shall introduce physical exercise in all our centres. We shall take part in all social activities collectively.

The Grameen Banks' resources consist of (i) share capital, (ii) deposits, (iii) contribution from members in the form of various funds, and (iv) borrowings from international agencies and the Bangladesh Bank.

The Bangladesh Grameen Bank has an unique approach to providing credit to the rural poor. It imposes a strict discipline on the borrowers as well as bank staff. The management also services the poorest of the poor in the rural areas who would, otherwise, have not been eligible for credit from other institutions

In an Islamic country, women have less rights than the men but the Grameen Bank has recognized their worth as individuals and as reliable instruments in the fight against rural poverty. When women become income-earners, the incremental income is systematically oriented towards increasing family well-being, which is not true of the male earners. This feature of intra-household distribution of incremental income and well-being is the basis for preference of women borrowers. The driving force behind the success of the experiment was the Founder Managing Director, Dr. Muhammad Yunus. The success of the project was largely due to the dedication of Dr. Yunus who nursed the project since its inception (K.G. Karmarkar, 2005).

SELF-HELP GROUP: NATIONAL SCENARIO

In India Self-help groups are formed by institutions of both government and non-government for various purposes, but the principal objective lies in the promotion of sustainable livelihood of rural masses through collective saving and self-employment activities. Both organizations promote the SHG formation and its activities with a view to utilize their services as the agents of implementing programmes of rural development.

The system is designed as a tool to empower the rural women in crosshead level. Social, economic and political empowerments of women are the basic requirements for their holistic development which is mainly focused in the national policy for empowerment of women 2001 under other action programmes of Government of India. When women participate freely in social, economic and political activities, they can acquire talents to increase their capabilities. The capability theory of living standard (Sen, 1987) holds that "income, commodities and wealth" do not ensure a decent living standard to their owners. It is the aggregate of certain capabilities like: (1) capability to live long, (2) capability to avoid illiteracy, (3) capability to be free from hunger and undernourishment, and (4) capability to enjoy personal liberty and freedom provides a decent standard of living. Human Development Report (UNDP, 1993).

Kamala Bhasin mentioned that some governments, UN organizations and NGOs have made special efforts to recruit women and train them for senior positions; and to make organizations, their policies, rules and work culture more women-friendly. Special gender indicators have been developed to measure the success of programmes aimed at women's empowerment and gender equality.

For making development more gender sensitive, government policies now increasingly emphasise qualitative inputs, focusing on inculcating self-confidence among women; generating awareness about their rights; and training them for economic activity and employment. Efforts to improve women's access to critical inputs and productive resources such as land, houses and trees through joint or individual titles have been expanded to include support through credit (or small scale capital), marketing, training in skills/ management and technology. Developing women's organizations is now accepted as an effective strategy for promoting women's empowerment.

GOVERNMENT PROGRAMMES FOR SELF-HELP GROUPS

Organizing self-help group is given at most priority in many developing countries like India. The self-help groups are receiving supports of different kinds of including finance from the government, non-government and international agencies.

Self-Help Groups system is designed so as to effective in empowering the rural women tackle poverty. Economic, social and political empowerment of women is one of the basis requirements for their development which has been strongly emphasized by regional perspective plans for women, 1988, other policies of the government including policy for empowerment of women 2001 and plan of nation for empowerment of women 2003-04, each one emphasizes ensuring women their rightful place in the society by empowering them on agents of social economic change and development. Only when women participate freely in economic activities partly outside home, they can control over circumstances to income their capabilities. Self-Help Groups provide appropriate forms for this purpose. SHG creates enabling environment for the members to become self-dependent, self-reliant and who it serves on a consulting forms for members for their social, psychological and economic problem (developing self-confidence, self-esteem capacity building and leadership qualities among the members).

The Government of India is committed to the welfare of women through empowering them which is acknowledged from: "to adopt an integrated approach, towards empowering women through effective conveyance of existing services, financial and human resources, and infrastructure in both women specific and women-related sectors". With a view to fulfilling such commitment the Government of India has been implementing policies for women development. Having realized the importance of Self-Help Groups in the process of uplifting the social, economic and political status of women, the central government has been framing policies for them. State governments have also followed the policies of central government.

In India, Mysore Rehabilitation and Development Agency (MYRADA), a Non-Government Organisation (NGO) has taken the lead of organizing the "CREDIT MANAGEMENT GROUPS" based on the concept of Self-Help Groups on a pilot basis in the year 1987 for which the NABARD had extended its ready support to evolve the innovations in the rural credit delivery system. Self-Help Groups serves as appropriate forum for the women members to discuss their feelings experience and needs freely. The SHG members gain confidence esteem and strength as a member working under the umbrella of self-help groups. The SHG members work together for the individual benefit as well as the group benefit and also for the village development. Self-Help Groups provide a platform to implement other government programmes in channelising the services to beneficiaries in a proper way. The Self-Help Groups paves a way to start into generating activities in a collective action. The self-help group deliver the timely help to satisfy their consumption credit and production credit needs and also releases the members out of the clutches of moneylenders. The self-help group also express their voice against the violence against women.

NABARD-SHG Bank Linkage Programme

In India, NABARD has been functioning as a catalyst in providing the necessary impetus for accelerating the growth of SHG linkage programme with the policy support from the Govt. of India and the Reserve Bank of India. The 'SHG-Bank Linkage Programme' is an important step to address the massive task of mainstreaming the very poor and the underprivileged with the formal banking system. A dedicated team of development professionals of NABARD, spanning the country in more than 380 locations with its district, state and corporate level offices, tirelessly work towards this goal. They work hand in hand with their partners in development.

The banking system in India is well known for its phenomenal outreach. Its legendary network fans out to the most remote rural pockets in the country. Yet, the formal banking services were out of bounds for the very poor, much to the chagrin of the policy-makers who created this large infrastructure over the past four decades. It was clear that the challenge was not in further creation of formal institutions to deliver microfinance services to the poor in the rural areas. The existing banking network of more than 150,000 rural outlets ensured the physical availability of such infrastructure. The need was to put in place a sub-system as a corollary to the existing banking network, which was at once cost effective and user-friendly for both banks, and the very poor. This way, the poor could relate to the banks in a better manner, and the banks, in turn, could consider banking with them as a business proposition. The challenge, therefore, was to link the poor in very large numbers to the formal banking sector, in a sustainable and cost effective manner.

The SHG-Bank Linkage Programme in India, as it is now popularly known, has emerged as the largest microfinance outreach programme in the World, and is also the most cost effective and fastest growing microfinance initiative the world over. An SHG has an average size of about 15 people from a homogeneous class. They come together for addressing their common problems. They are encouraged to make voluntary thrift on a regular basis. They use this pooled resources to make small interest bearing loans to their members. The process helps them imbibe the essentials of financial intermediation including prioritization of needs, setting terms and conditions, and accounts keeping. This gradually builds financial discipline in all of them. They also learn to handle resources of a size that is much beyond individual capacities of any of them. The SHG members begin to appreciate that resources are limited and have a cost. Once the groups show this mature financial behaviour, banks are encouraged to make loans to the SHG in certain multiples of the accumulated savings of the SHG. The bank loans are given without any collateral and at market interest rates. The groups continue to decide the terms of loans to their own members. Since the groups' own accumulated savings are part and parcel of the aggregate loans made by the groups to their members, peer pressure ensures timely repayments.

Benefits of Self-Help Groups

For members

- Discuss and help each other to solve common problems.
- Collect and use own savings to make interest bearing small loans to each other.
- Learn basics of financial intermediation.
- Learn to appreciate others' needs and priorities their own needs.
- Start handling resources of a size much beyond their individual capacities.
- Realise that resources are scarce and that they have a cost.
- Learn that repayment is not difficult, with regular savings habit.
- Use peer pressure as an effective substitute for collateral security.
- Win the confidence of the formal banking system through mature financial behaviour, leading to further access to need-based funds.
- Learn to interact with the external environment in a meaningful way, leading to increased self-esteem and confidence.

For Banks

- Benefit from reduced transaction costs through economies of scale.
- Learn to externalize credit supervision and servicing to the NGOs or to the Self-Help Groups themselves.
- Benefit from mobilization of small savings through groups, gaining access to low-cost funds.
- Accept peer pressure within the Self-Help Groups as an excellent substitute for collateral securities, leading to more than 95% repayments.
- Get timely repayments leading to faster recycling of funds.
- Recognize Self-Help Groups as the appropriate medium for expansion of business of rural branches for wider coverage of clientele.

- Recognize the prospects of 'ripple effect' in quality among their clientele.
- Build goodwill among the rural clientele.
- Benefit from full refinance facility from NABARD for better fund management.

For NGOs

- Find Self-Help Groups as complimentary to their core functions.
- Use the synergy of social and economic programmes for better impact on the poor.
- Deepen and widen the outreach to the poor through 'credit plus' approach.
- Gain recognition as socio-economic change agents.
- Use the avenue for performing financial intermediation in underbanked areas.
- Act as meaningful agents between banks and the poor.
- Perform the role of propagators of innovative financial services delivery approaches.

The SHG-Bank Linkage Programme was provided to 18,29,847 Self-Help Groups, the cumulative bank loan disbursed for Rs. 83,191 million and the cumulative refinance drawn by banks for Rs. 37,414 million.

General

- Conceptualized and introduced the pilot phase of SHG-Bank Linkage Programme.
- Contributes to conducive policy framework.
- Value addition to the programme by developing and sharing different types of conceptual inputs for the stakeholders.
- Making available on large scale capacity building inputs.
- Fund support for expendable and loan funding needs of participating agencies.
- Holds training consultations, supports stakeholders in training interventions.
- Supports banks to act as Self-Help Promoting Institutions.
- Closely monitors the programme through provincial and district-level forums.

- Develops region specific strategies.
- Conducts goal-oriented project planning interventions for field-level staff for better appreciation and solving of location specific problems.
- Encourages evolution of intermediary structures.

Regarding Promotional Grant Support the NABARD has sanctioned Rs. 275.48 lakhs for promotion of 31,960 Self-Help Groups to 62 Co-operative banks, 105 RRBs have been sanctioned Rs. 314.74 lakhs for promotion of 39,735 Self-Help Groups, 1,312 NGOs have been sanctioned Rs. 2,176.55 lakhs for promotion of 1,50,088 Self-Help Groups, 17 Individual Rural Volunteers (IRVs) have been sanctioned Rs. 75.32 lakhs for promotion of 5775 Self-Help Groups and Rs. 48.94 lakhs has been released to Farmers' Clubs for promotion of 11,245 Self-Help Groups.

As Training Support is concerned the NABARD supported 5,111 training programmes for training 1,68,032 bank officials, 976 training programmes supported for training 26,919 NGO officials, 90 programmes supported for training 2,822 trainers from banks, 746 programmes supported for training 34,247 Government Officials, 14,780 programmes supported for training 6,79,165 members of Self-Help Groups and 130 programmes for training the Elected members of PRIs conducted covering 5,026 participants.

The Promotion of micro-Enterprise among members of mature Self-Help Groups, establishment of Grain banks, associating local rural volunteers as book writers for Self-Help Groups, automation of book keeping in Self-Help Groups and a pilot project on 'e-Grama' for establishing Village Information Centres are the innovative pilot projects carried out by NABARD.

SELF-HELP GROUPS IN TAMIL NADU

Tamil Nadu Corporation for Development of Women Ltd.

Tamil Nadu Corporation for Development of Women Ltd., incorporated in the year 1983 in Chennai. The Corporation was set-up in order to focus on women's empowerment, particularly economic empowerment, with a focus on those in disadvantaged situations.

Tamil Nadu Women's Development Project started on an

experimental basis in Dharmapuri district in 1989 with external funding from International Fund for Agricultural Development (IFAD) received its first growth thrust in 1991-92 expanding to Salem and South Arcot districts immediately followed by Madurai and Ramanathapuram districts in 1993. The expansion has continued till today and is popularly called Mahalir Thittam. This is a unique partnership between (a) a Government agency, Dew; (b) Non-Governmental Organisations (NGOs); and (c) banks. The project is implemented through a network of women's Self-Help Groups established and nurtured with NGO support at the village level.

As on 30.9.2001 the coverage stands at 16,76,733 lakhs women enrolled in 97,394 Self-Help Groups in rural and urban areas. The partner NGOs is 315 in number. With expansion in coverage the process of NGO selection has been streamlined. There are prescribed formats for pre-selection application and inspections. Team inspections are carried out. It is important to select only those NGOs who have demonstrated certain minimum strength, commitment and orientation. The number of banks extending credit has increased to 43. Commercial and co-operative banks have also been brought into the fold of SHG lending.

The core of the Tamil Nadu Women's Development Project is the formation of cohesive women's Self-Help Groups where rural women are encouraged to pool their savings on a regular basis, however small they may be, into a group common fund. This common fund grows not only through individual contributions, but also by rotation of the money among group members through internal lending. This activity also teaches the members interest calculation and the importance of repayment, thus contributing to financial disciplines. Even without institutional loans, this has contributed to considerable relief from local moneylenders. Regularity in savings, rather than the amount and internal rotation are the basis of group strength. By September 2001 the aggregate group level savings of the over 16 lakh women added up to a handsome amount of Rs.124.40 crores.

Increased focus on the poorest and the most disadvantaged women has been brought about, with preference to widows, destitute, divorcees, physically handicapped women and women belonging to the weaker sections. The SC/ST percentage among members has been growing and stands at 46%, as on 30.9.2001 quality an implementation is the guiding principle.

Training is a very important activity under the project. The groups are trained through NGOs and pave the way to create awareness and motivate the members to realize their strengths and weaknesses and their potential. Gradually, they become more conscious for their capabilities and start exhibiting them through their action plans and programme.

Monitoring is a vital tool in implementing project activities to achieve the desired impact on the target groups. Creation of databases, ensuring quality and reliability, regular updating, continuous two-way information flow and feedback which are the basis for Monitoring and Evaluation. Another area of vital attention has been the need to introduce and strengthen the concept of participatory and self-monitoring amongst SHG members. As a first measure, institutionalization of the monthly Block-level coordination committee meeting (BLCC) has been a vital step forward. BLCC functionaries are trained to review the performance of member Self-Help Groups at the BLCC meetings. The main function of the Monitoring and Evaluation division is the receipt and consolidation of reports from all plus and to have first hand information of the project progress. The group grading exercise is taken regularly. They serve not only as an assessment of the level at which the groups are on a gradation scale of A to D based on specific indicators but it also serves as a tool for participatory Self-evaluation exercise.

Grading of NGOs working under the project and the Plus are carried out once in 6 months periodically. This is done to identify weak NGOs, with a poor track, and to improve the delivery of services to the ultimate beneficiaries. Grading of NGOs assess themselves and submit their reports to PIU. A committee sits with the NGO and assesses the report.

Mature groups ready to absorb bank loans are linked with financial institutions to avail credit. As on 31.03.2006, 2,16,496 Self-Help Groups have received linkages with institutional credit access of Rs. 1,76,524 lakhs for various rural-based activities. Their credit-worthiness has been proved beyond doubt and repayment is largely on schedule, with overdues being an exception. The loans are disbursed and recovered through the group and the groups take responsibility for repayment. In turn, the group extends credit to the members, after group consensus. The members thus avail loans for income generating activities of their choice. The lending and recovery procedures have thus built in safety in ensuring prompt payment through peer pressure of group members reinforced by "SHG credit guidelines" and grading of groups which have become streamlined over the years. The major credit sources are SGSY, NABARD, RMK/NGO loan, and SJSRY, etc.

Cluster Level Federation is a democratic body formed with certain number of Self-Help Groups functioning in a specific geographical area in close proximity with the objective of uniting such Self-Help Groups for common cause, especially for achieving those causes that an individual SHG would find difficult to do. In short, the SHG federation has to be necessarily of Self-Help Groups, by Self-Help Groups and for Self-Help Groups and it is a stop to achieve long-term sustainability of the groups through mutual support and cooperation.

The Corporation funds specific Vocational Training Programmes (VTPs) for economically disadvantaged women in rural as well as urban areas of Tamil Nadu. Funds out of the corporation's surplus as well as state budgetary resources are utilized. Moreover, Government of India provides funds for training and training-*cum*-production centers through funds from the Norwegian Agency for International Development (NORAD) that is channeled through this corporation. Similarly, funds are available under support to employment programme (STEP).

This Corporation undertakes the task of pre-scrutiny and processing of all proposals before sanction either at the corporation level or by Government of India. A list of expert monitors has also been suggested by the government of India to help in the monitoring of the projects. There is a continuous endeavor to identify occupations currently in demand in order to improve the marketable skills available to women.

Women's recreation has traditionally not received official recognition as part of any development programme under government. Normally, in our society, men have several places to meet and discuss matters of interest, play games, etc. Such a facility is not easily available to women, especially among the poorer sections of society. Most development programmes recognize needs for nutrition, health, education, water supply, income generation. There is no explicit recognition of the need for recreation for women by itself. This innovative scheme identifies this gap and attempts to make a beginning by filling it.

The centers are located in pre-school noon meals programme (NMP) centers or other suitable public buildings where Self-Help Groups are active. On seeing the response to the scheme it is proposed to set-up WRCs in all panchayat villages throughout the state in a phased manner over a period of five years. A sum of Rs. 3,000 per center is provided for initially equipping the center with materials like plastic mat, newspapers, magazines, games, transistor-*cum*-tape recorder, audio tapes, tube light fittings, plug point, storage box with lock and electricity charges. In addition a sum of Rs. 1,070 per center is provided for recurring expenses.

A separate society, by name "MUTRAM" has been formed to bring out a monthly magazine of the same name, for the benefit of SHG women. The society was formed in April 1998. IFAD had also provided a grant of US $ 30,000 to MUTRAM society towards building up a corpus fund for ensuring continuous uninterrupted publication of the magazine. The interest from this corpus is being utilized to bring out the magazine. UNICEF has contributed Rs. 2 lakhs during 1999-2000. Sofar monthly Mutram issues have been published monthly promptly till date from May 1998. TNCDW is publishing a quarterly newsletter called 'Microfinance News Letter' for the benefit of bankers, NGOs and other players in the field to share their experiences in the field of 'Microfinance'.

The main partners of the corporation in social development process are NGOs. It is very important for us to build the capacity of small and medium sized NGOs to enable them to work better for benefit of the Self-Help Groups. Further, 2001 has been declared as the International year of the volunteer. Hence, in order to promote active performance by both NGOs and individual volunteer for benefit of society. NGO volunteer resource center (NVRC) is being setup for capacity building of NGOs, volunteer promotion, data exchange, networking and documentation.

Entrepreneurship skill training is being undertaken by several agencies like THADCO, TABCEDCO, Directorate of Industries and commerce and TNCDW. Government of Tamil Nadu has given a massive thrust for EDP training for women and 5 lakh women will be trained during (2001-06) through the following departments:

Rural Development, Industries and commerce, TAHDCO, TNCDW, Tamil Nadu slum clearance board, agriculture, backward classes and minorities welfare, sericulture, TNCDW has been appointed as the nodal agency. The TNCDW will take up this Entrepreneurship Development Programme training in respect of 1 lakh economically weaker SHG women members who have obtained external credit linkages. As poor, semi-literate women need specially designed training methods and materials, and since a very large number is proposed to be covered, a training manual for the use of EDP training has been developed by TNCDW and it has been approved as the syllabus for the EDP training to 5 lakh women in 2001-06 a systematic training of trainers has also been undertaken who, in turn, will train the women. Woman who does not possess any skill and choose a particular trade during the EDP will be assisted in getting the required skill training also. After training assistance will be provided for credit linkages with nationalized banks/financial institutions through the respective Self-Help Groups. These trainers will in turn train potential entrepreneurs among women's groups with business and technical skill for women.

Development councils are being constituted at panchayat-level with representatives of Self-Help Groups in villages and supported by Panchayat Presidents, Grama Sewaks, Anganwadi Workers, VHNs and NGOs. These councils will act as panchayat level teams for supporting economic, social and democratic empowerment of women. They will help eligible Self-Help Groups to access external credit in close coordination with the Rural Development Department and local bank branches enabling to become increasingly self-reliant. The development councils will also work for convergence service of various departments with Self-Help Groups enabling better services at field-level.

The decade long experience of Dew, banks and NGOs in working together has culminated in the convergence process with other Government departments so that: (a) there are realistic expectations about the process and outcomes, and (b) the mistakes made earlier are not repeated all over again. In Tamil Nadu, already, the Mahalir Thittam scheme is being converged with the RD Department's SGSY, SGSRY scheme of MAWS to bring about a convergence of services and approach to avoid the very same families and women being approached by multiple agencies in conflicting ways. Similarly, for the benefit of SC/ST families, some TAHDCO schemes are also being made available to the Self-Help Groups. This way, not only can the learning under Mathi be made available to other schemes contributing to improved implementation, but also some of the expenditure can be booked under central funding and thus contribute to budgetary economics for the state government. Convergence with directorate of Indian medicine, watershed programs, health, agriculture, TNINP, labour department are currently being focused.

Group Formation

Group Formation will be preceded by a village-level household survey, which will provide the base-line data. This should be conducted by Non-Governmental Organizations, for which techniques like Social Mapping, Participatory Rural Appraisal (PRA)/ Participatory Learning & Action (PLA) and Wealth Ranking should be used to identify the poorest habitations. By and larger the groups must be mixed groups, being composed of members from the different communities as far as possible. Also having more than one member of the same family in the same SHG is to be strictly avoided, as this would lead to bias in decision-making and poor group dynamics.

Group Meetings

The group must meet every week for savings and repayment collections and every fortnight for discussing all other matters in addition to savings and repayment.

Group meetings need to be conducted with a certain discipline in relation to regularity, time and items to be discussed. There needs to be a fixed day/date every week/10 days, on which day and time the meeting is to be conducted. Any member, including the animator/representative, who without prior intimation to the group, either does not turn up or turns up late, is to pay a fine as imposed by the group on such member.

After jointly taking the Mahalir Thittam pledge, the SHG meeting has to commence with certain items such as savings, rotation of sangha funds, bank loans and repayments, social and community action programmes, must be discussed in every meeting without fail. Further, there needs to be special agenda, or set of items to be discussed in each meeting. The monthly newsletter "Mutram" needs to be read in every meeting and topics discussed.

Transparency in SHG transactions is very essential. Loud reading of the minutes (resolutions) and fund balances of the SHG by the animator or any member should be done at the end of the meeting itself and again at the beginning of the next meeting, so that, members do not claim ignorance of certain decisions or financial transactions of the SHG.

Group Maintenance Fund

To supplement the group fund, an amount of Rs. 15 per member is to be collected initially on group formation, which will be in addition to the group savings. This will cover the cost of stationery, rubber stamps, register, postage, etc. After six months another one time collection of Rs. 10 is also to be made.

The member of the group should also contribute a minimum of Rs. 2 per month per member as Group Maintenance Fund. This could be utilized for certain minor purposed like TA for bank visits, purchase of stationery items, etc.

Group Savings

SHG members must be encouraged to save as much as each can without it being a uniform amount for all. Self-Help Groups starting with fixed savings can be motivated to switch to optional savings (Subject to a minimum saving). This is especially relevant as most SHG members have seasonal employment and can make up for poorer savings during lean season with higher savings during employment season by adopting optional savings. Regular weekly saving is the most important factor that determines the speed of growth leading to quicker sustainability.

Rotation of Group Funds

All savings and common fund would be rotated amongst the members at rates of interest to be decided by the group. It usually varies between 2% and 3% p.m. To whom the sangha loan should be given is also a group decision. This sangha loan would enable the members to meet their small consumption and productive needs without having to go to the money-lender or bank or co-operative society. Internal loans should be prioritized and differential rates of interest could be charged for emergency loans, as distinct from loans for income generating activities and family functions.

Self-Help Groups should be motivated to completely (100%) rotate their savings preferably from the first month of their formation. It should be noted that group cohesion and understanding develops only because the members learn to prioritise demands *vs.* availability in the spirit of mutual give and take. Any delay in internal rotation will only delay development of the SHG, besides driving the SHG members back into the clutches of the local moneylender.

Animators and Representatives

The animators will be form the local village and must necessarily be a resident of the village. The animator should preferably be literate and must possess certain leadership qualities. She must be in a position to take on the role of a trainer for the group members in certain aspects of their daily life and group functioning, based on the training that would be given to her. In short, she must be a role model and a change agent for the groups and for the village as a whole. It is therefore necessary that she should not be defaulter of bank loans herself. She should also not be an office-bearer of any other organization, so that there is greater loyalty and commitment to the SHG. She should be the locus for free and democratic functioning of the SHG.

Two Representatives are nominated by the SHG from amongst members, rotated on a yearly basis, to ensure carrying out certain tasks of group.

The animator's position must be rotated amongst the representatives once every two years. She will facilitate a smooth switchover of responsibilities in the above process. She will also assist the representatives to learn the role of the animator to facilitate handling over of responsibilities as and when required.

Opening of Accounts, Operation and Accessing Institutional Credit

Self-Help Groups should immediately open bank accounts on formation in order to ensure safer and transparent transactions. This account may be opened in any bank of their choice depending upon their convenience and proximity since the service areas norms are not applicable to the SHG loans being advanced by nationalized banks with NABARD re-finance assistance. This is an important activity and will help in safe handling of SHG funds, avoiding.

It is recommended that every SHG member go by rotation to the bank in order to learn banking transactions and to ensure exposure and development of all SHG members. This also results in SHG transactions and accounts becoming transparent to all members. This also results in SHG transactions and accounts becoming transparent to all members, lessening possibilities of malpractice.

Books of accounts and registers to be maintained by Self-Help Groups. The following books and registers have to be maintained in every group:

1. Attendance register
2. Minutes book
3. Savings ledger
4. Loan ledger
5. General ledger
6. Cash book
7. Individual pass book
8. Receipt book
9. Payment vouchers

The above books and registers will have to be maintained and updated on a regular basis for which the primary responsibility will rest with the animator. The first set of books and registers will be supplied by the PIU, NGOs may ensure that the double entry book-keeping system suggested is followed strictly.

Training

Since this project is basically a human resource development project, training is being given top priority. Certain topics of training will be imparted through the animators/representatives to the groups while some other topics will be imparted directly to the groups.

In addition to regular training, refresher training will also be provided to the animators and representatives.

Communication

As an aid to sustainability, there should be an effective communication component. As an essential part of it, there would be a periodical newsletter for sharing of experiences. The newsletter would be at the state-level. The magazine MUTRAM has completed 17 months of successful existence.

In addition, video films would be produced for documentation of the project. NGOs are requested to build up effective communication teams for reaching out awareness messages to illiterate SHG members. Awareness songs and streets plays should also be used during training or BLCC sessions to convey messages. PIUs will convene half-yearly communicator's meets at the district-level to effect exchange of valuable communication material between NGOs.

Economic Assistance

The groups can receive economic assistance, if any, from the Tamil Nadu Corporation for Development of Women Ltd. They can also access economic assistance under any scheme of Government, such as SGSY, SJSRY, TAHDCO, TABCEDCO, etc.

No economic assistance is to be given till the group is cohesive enough to receive it. This would be assessable after a minimum period of 6 months after group formation.

Subsidy Administration

Any economic assistance scheme, like SGSY, TAHDCO, KVIC, etc., in the project having a subsidy component has to be administered through the group. No individual subsidies are to be given. Subsidy is to be given to the group and used to enhance the capital base of the SHG. It should not be divided among the members.

This subsidy is a good repayment bonus. Only after 100% repayment of loan-*cum*-interest, the subsidy, which is kept as a fixed deposit, would be given to the group. Hence, subsidy is not adjusted against the loan, and full economic assistance is treated as loan.

Annual Auditing

Groups accounts be audited annually by engaging a local qualified auditor at the village/cluster itself. The groups should meet the audit cost. Groups should follow-up and rectify the deficiencies pointed out by the auditor and ensure that lapses to not recur. NGO should facilitate this process. NGOs should ensure that SHG accounts are audited in April and May of every year promptly by arrangement with standard auditors. The auditors' report should be in Tamil and should be read out in the subsequent SHG meeting, minuted and pasted in the minute's book. NGOs may consider making audit a participatory process with presence of SHG members.

Block-Level Coordination Committee

The monthly BLCC meetings are to be conduced by SHG women representatives.

The BLCC meetings are to elect a couple of functionaries to convene meetings—may be called Secretary/Jt. Secretary or Governor/Jt. Governor or Representatives of the CLF. BLCC meetings are to be conducted by the SHG women themselves (preferably in the usual SHG fashion—without chairs) with the NGO/PIU staff sitting outside the circle in the side. (Mahalir Thittam Working Manual)

Rural Development Banking—Bank of Madura Model

The quest of synthesizing the structure and objectives of its rural credit operations has lead to the promotion of Self-Help Groups (SHGs) as an alternate mechanism for delivery of rural credit. The Rural Development Division has been established on 1995 and has accepted promotion of Self-Help Groups particularly for rural poor women on its mainstream of business as a conscious decision after much deliberation. SHG is now considered as the most ideal vehicle for overall socio-economic development of the rural areas. Based on the experience gained from promotion of various types of Self-Help Groups, the bank has evolved its own model of SHG, the prime objective of which is to improve the socio-economic conditions of rural families as well as the development of rural entrepreneurship.

Objectives

- To create awareness and provide basic education to rural women,
- To inculcate savings habit and enable the rural poor to multiply the funds available with them and create an atmosphere conducive to mutual help and togetherness,
- To identify and upgrade the skills available with the rural women in order to increase the level of income generation, and

- On a macro-level, the model is aimed at converting the rural area as producing centers instead of merely centers of conception.

At present Bank of Madura was taken over by ICICI bank and implementing the same rural development banking at the same manner.

SELF-HELP GROUPS: BOON TO HOLISTIC DEVELOPMENT

Self-Help Groups are proved to be very fruitful not only for the empowerment of women but also for the holistic community development. The role of Self-Help Groups are very vital to implement all the developmental programmes to fulfil its real objectives.

Self-Help Groups: Convergence of Services

All Government and Non-Government agencies working in a co-ordinated fashion, catch fully understanding the others' roles, speaking the same language, ensuring complementarity, avoiding and preventing overlaps and adding value to each other's work, for facilitating sustainable linkages for the poor.

They represent women who need to be brought into the mainstream of public participation. Self-Help Groups are a band of willing volunteers sensitized to social and community action, when compared to individual citizens. They are organized, united and therefore effective. Self-Help Groups are capable of mobilising the community. They represent the poor, the depressed and the village community or citizen at large.

Role of Self-Help Groups

- Parent Teacher Associations (PTA) can be strengthened with participation of Self-Help Groups and NGO facilitation.
- Self-Help Groups can participate in health programmes as volunteers.
- Self-Help Groups to act as tools for community participation in the Child Welfare Center (CWC) including maintenance and supervision of CWCs. Anganwadi Workers (AWWs) to be trained by MaThi for SHG facilitation

- Self-Help Groups are sensitised to the need for stopping crime against women. Self-Help Groups are capable of handling dowry and cruelty against women.
- Self-Help Groups can serve as friends of police to prevent violence against women.

Women Self-Help Groups and Sanitation

Total Sanitation Campaign under Central Rural Sanitation Programme was introduced in 1999 in India to replace the earlier supply driver, top down allocation programme. Total Sanitation Campaign in a paradigm shift to demand responsive, participatory and community-led programme using campaign approach. In 2002, TSC was implemented in Ramnad district. Tamilnadu with objective of construction and delivery of 80,000 low cost toilets in all households below poverty line using appropriate technology.

The Centre for Women's Studies of Alagappa University, Karaikudi was identified as the District Coordinating Agency to carryout IEC (Information, Education and Communication) activities, rural sanitary mart and Production Centers, construction of Individual Household Latrines (IHHLs), Woman sanitary complexes and school sanitation. The scheme was successfully implemented with maximum result in a short period of time mainly by utilizing the services of SHG women. The Ramnad Modal was suggested and should be replicated in other districts of Tamilnadu. This is a comment by state government of Tamilnadu. For the success of the project, the centre adopted an integrated multi-Sectoral approach for effective and efficient implementation of the project by involving the participation of the agencies like District Rural Development Agency, Block Administration, line departments, (Health, Education, TWAD, Social Welfare, Tamilnadu Corporation for development of women Ltd.), Non-Governmental organizations, Panchayatraj institutions and Self-Help Group women. Among all these agencies very prominent role was played by SHG women in this project. The target of 80,000 IHHLS were completed and started utilization was achieved only because the involvement of SHG women.

Women Self-Help Group and Environment

There is a growing realization throughout India that the

environmental problems resulting from human activities pose a threat to sustainability of life. For the development of a nation, it needs both economical and ecological sustainability. The attainment of sustainability development is closely related with preservation and conservation of environment. As the population increased, more natural resources were consumed in the process of satisfying the rapidly growing needs of the habitat. The population explosion has decimated natural resources, promoted mass migration. This has led deterioration in the quality of life and increased the pollution. The term pollution refers to alteration of surrounding wholly as largely as a byproduct of human's action. Too much of human interference with nature has greatly changed the natural assets. Every developmental activity has impact on the environment. It is necessary to make the population to realize the enormity of problem of environment degradation.

With 16% of the world population and 2.4% of the world's land area, India has a population density of 300 per square kilometer. Combined with rapid population growth, this has led to environmental degradation of natural resources. The Platform for Action emphasized that women have an important role to play in the development of sustainable and ecologically sound patterns of consumption and production as well as practical approaches to natural resource management. This was recognized at the United Nations Conference on environment and development 1992, and reflected in agenda 21. Women's experiences and contributions to maintaining an ecologically sound environment must therefore be central to the agenda for the twenty-first Century.

In response, the government has begun to promote an active and visible policy of accepting women's role in all environmental policies and programmes. The lack of sufficient recognition and support for women's contributions to conservation and management of natural resource and safeguarding the environment is being addressed. Women's participation in movements in different parts of the country, from the demands of women from West Bengal for land rights during the struggle for land reforms in 1979, to the historical Chipko movement in Uttar Pradesh, has been very significant. Much of the environmental legislation which recognizes the relationship of human beings with their environment have their roots in agitation and demands by women's groups.

Conservation of the Environment

Conservation of our bio-diversity is very much a part of our history. After independence, the most significant legislation on bio-diversity conservation was the 42nd amendment of the Indian constitution passed in 1976, making protection and improvement of the environment and safeguarding of forest and wildlife one of the directive principles of state policy. The National forest policy of 1988 aims to have at least one-third land under forest cover. The Environment Action Plan, 1993 mentions conservation of land and sustainable utilization of bio-diversity in selected, ecosystems as a top priority along with eco-development. Governmental programmes for the promotion of afforestation, wasteland development, fuel and fodder production, conservation of minor forest producers and aerial seeding are being further strengthened under the Ninth Plan. The major environment problem in India, as identified in the Ninth-Five Year Plan related to air and water pollution, degradation of common property resources threat to biological diversity, solid waste disposal and sanitation.

Participation Approach to Environmental Protection

The participation approach to environmental protection is now being greatly emphasized in many countries. The most important requirement for sustainable development is the protection of forest and bio-diversity, soil conservation, protection of common resources, population control, restoration of tanks, rural energy movement, popularization of environment-friendly agricultural practices, etc. The participatory to environmental protection can be strengthened with the help of Self-Help Group women. Self-Help Groups have got potential today with respect to increasing awareness among the rural people day-to-day affair such as safe drinking water and sanitation, improvement of health education, etc. The concept of SHG serves to underline the principle "for the people, by the people and of the people". Self-Help group is a small economically homogeneous and affinity group of rural poor which voluntarily agrees to contribute to a common food to be lent to its members of per group decision which works for group solidarity, self and group awareness, social, economic and political empowerment in the way of democratic functioning.

The degradation of environment can be checked with the

intervention of rural women Self-Help Groups. Since it is being the major programme with coverage of the large rural population, Self-Help Groups need to be utilized to impart environmental education to women. To bring ecological balance and to promote bio-diversity, the SHG Women have to be educated on afforestation, soil conservation, watershed movement, rural sanitation, waste management, etc. and also to enhance them as management of natural disaster.

The new programme has been developed to provide assistance to rural women through the erstwhile Integrated Rural Development Programme, now merged under the Swarna Jayanthi Gram Swarojgar Yojana (SGSY) scheme to raise nurseries in forest lands. Rural women living below the poverty line will be provided with financial assistance under this programme and receive subsidies and credit for raising nurseries was an opportunity for self-employment and income generation. The beneficiaries will be provided with technology-based packages of nursery practices by the forest departments and various forest research institutes in the country. Measures to provide clean and safe drinking water, which started in the early 80's have continued through the coordinated efforts of organizations like the National Institute of communicable Diseases, the Rajiv Gandhi National Drinking Water Mission and Institutional organizations like WHO and UNICEF, State Health and Public Health of Environment departments. The eradication of guinea worm is a good example of such efforts.

Disaster Management

India is one of the areas in the world, most afflicted by natural disasters. The Maharashtra Government's Disaster Management Plan, introduced in August 1998, is one of the first multi-disaster response mechanisms in the country, evolved from the state government's management of the 1993 earthquake in Latur, which affected more than 2500 villages in 13 districts, it flattered 55,000 houses in 63 villages killing 2000 people. The state government recognized that the response of communities, especially that of the women to post-disaster aid, could build an effective part for transition from disaster to development. As a part of state policy metropolis moments/ women's groups were mobilized in over 500 villages to work as Samvad Sohayaks or village assistants in the reconstruction on programme. Over 1000 women were trained on village assistants to supervise earthquake resistant construction. Women also initiated Gram Sabhas and linked up with Gram Panchayat members to solve problems like water transport. Today there is a Mahila Mandal in every village and credit societies have mushroomed in all the districts to support the efforts of the Mahila Mandal who are involved in the areas of health, education and animal husbandry.

The success of rural sanitation programme by utilizing the strength of Self-Help Group women can be a model for other schemes. Like that to bring ecological balance and to promote bio-diversity the services of SHG women could be utilized in remaining areas such as afforestation, soil conservation, watershed movement, waste management, etc. By involving the SHG women in environmental protection, the country will get both economical and ecological sustainability.

Thus, the concept of Self-Help Groups serves as a vital instrument to implement all developmental programmes for the holistic development of the nation.

2

Women Empowerment

- Concept of Empowerment
- National Mission for Empowerment of Women
- Measures of Empowerment
- Process of Women Empowerment
- Approaches for Women Empowerment
- Spheres of Women Empowerment

Empowerment refers to increasing the spiritual, political, social, educational, gender, or economic strength of individuals and communities. The term empowerment covers a vast landscape of meanings, interpretations, definitions and disciplines ranging from psychology and philosophy to the highly commercialized self-help industry and motivational sciences. Sociological empowerment often addresses members of groups that social discrimination processes have excluded from decision-making processes through, for example, discrimination based on disability, race, ethnicity, religion, or gender. Empowerment as a methodology is often associated with feminism: "Marginalized" refers to the overt or covert trends within societies whereby those perceived as lacking desirable traits or deviating from the group norms tend to be excluded by wider society and ostracized as undesirables.

Sometimes groups are marginalized by society at large, but governments are often unwitting or enthusiastic participants. For example, the U.S. government marginalized cultural minorities, particularly blacks, prior to the Civil Rights Act of 1964. This Act made it illegal to restrict access to schools and public places based on race. Equal opportunity laws which actively oppose such marginalization, allow increased empowerment to occur. They are also a symptom of minorities' and women's empowerment through lobbying.

Marginalized people who lack self-sufficiency become, at a minimum, dependent on charity, or welfare. They lose their self-confidence because they cannot be fully self-supporting. The opportunities denied them also deprive them of the pride of accomplishment which others, who have those opportunities, can develop for themselves. This in turn can lead to psychological, social and even mental health problems.

Empowerment is then the process of obtaining these basic opportunities for marginalized people, either directly by those people, or through the help of non-marginalized others who share their own access to these opportunities. It also includes actively thwarting attempts to deny those opportunities. Empowerment also includes encouraging, and developing the skills for, self-sufficiency, with a focus on eliminating the future need for charity or welfare in the individuals of the group. This process can be difficult to start and to implement effectively, but there are many examples of empowerment projects which have succeeded.

One empowerment strategy is to assist marginalized people to create their own non-profit organization, using the rationale that only the marginalized people, themselves, can know what their own people need most, and that control of the organization by outsiders can actually help to further entrench marginalization. Charitable organizations lead from outside of the community; for example, can disempowering the community by entrenching a dependence on charity or welfare. A non-profit organization can target strategies that cause structural changes, reducing the need for ongoing dependence. Red Cross, for example, can focus on improving the health of indigenous people, but does not have authority in its charter to install water-delivery and purification systems, even though the lack of such a system profoundly, directly and negatively impacts health. A non-profit composed of the indigenous people, however, could ensure their own organization does have such authority and could set their own agendas, make their own plans, seek the needed resources, do as much of the work as they can, and take responsibility —and credit—for the success of their projects.

Empowerment is the process of building capacities of creating an atmosphere, which enables people to fully utilize their creative potential in pursuance of quality of life. It also deeper and popularizes the democratic process. Empowerment gives women the capacity to influence decision-making process, planning, implementation and evaluation by integrating them into the political system. Empowerment has become a buzzword for last few decades. It has a number of connotations. Empowerment is a process by which the disempowered, or powerless, people can change their circumstances and begin to have control over their lives. More importantly empowerment means the way women think of themselves not as a victim of circumstances, but as architects of their destinies. Empowerment results in a change in the balance of power, in the living conditions, and in the relationships. Empowerment is a process, not a product. The outcome of empowerment would then be redistribution of power.

In short, empowerment is the process by which the powerless or disempowered gain greater control over the circumstances of their lives. It includes control over resources and decision-making. The resources over which control can be exercised fall into 5 broad categories:

1. Physical resources (land, water, forests);
2. Human resources (people, their bodies, their labor and skills);
3. Intellectual Resources (knowledge, information, ideas);
4. Financial resources (money, access to money); and
5. Control of Ideology (the ability to determine beliefs, values, and attitudes virtually control over ways of thinking and perceiving situations.

Empowerment is both individual and collective. The term empowerment refers to a range of activities from individual self-assertion to collective resistance protest and mobilization that challenge basic power relations. Women in the informal economy are socially and economically weak and vulnerable, and it is only by the process of coming together that they can be empowered. Thus, the goal of empowerment is to:

- Challenge sub-ordination.
- Transform the structures, systems and institutions which have supported inequality such as the family, caste and class system, religion, top down development models, etc.

CONCEPT OF EMPOWERMENT

Empowerment is the process of challenging existing power relations and of gaining greater control over the sources of power. The goals of women's empowerment are to challenge patriarchal ideology to transform the structures and institutions that reinforce and perpetuate gender discrimination and social inequality and to enable poor women to gain access to and control of both material and informational resources. It can change existing power relations by addressing itself to the three dimensions of material, human and intellectual resources. Empowerment cannot occur as a revolution but only as evolution. Empowerment means different things to different people. In recent years, much has been written about alternative, highly participatory, empowerment-oriented approaches to development. These are varied and they are not mutually exclusive (Tehranian, 1994).

The dictionary meaning of the term empowerment is to give power, to give them capacity to perform some physical or mental activity, to delegate authority, to give legal rights, to enable, to entitle, to endow (invest with powers). The most conspicuous feature of the term empowerment is that it contains the word 'power' by empowerment would be able to develop self-esteem, confidence realize that potential and enhance their collective bargaining.

The literary meaning of empowerment indicates that it is conferred on the root concept power. Then what is power, "power is the ability of one person or group to get another person or group to do something against their will. Power in relation to social, economic and political aspects indicates control over resources and decision-making" (Jo Rowland, 1997).

Batliwala defined that empowerment in broad sense covers aspects such as women's control over material and intellectual resources.

Sharma (1992) empowerment in its simplest form means redistribution of power that challenges the male dominance. This does not however mean that the empowerment process adopts and antagonists approach. It is only to enable women to supplement and coordinate with men. Empowerment is an active process of enabling women to realize their identity, potentiality and power in all spheres of their lives.

According to Srilatha Batliwala, "Power can be defined as control over resources, ideology and self, exercised in social, economic and political context among individuals and groups".

Sen and Batliwala (2000), defined "empowerment is the process by which the powerless gain greater control over the circumstances of their lives. It includes both control over resources and over ideology...(includes, in addition to extrinsic control) a growing intrinsic capability, greater self-confidence, and an inner transformation of one's consciousness that enables one to overcome external barriers".

According to Adams (1996), "Empowerment is the means by which individuals, groups and communities to take control of their circumstances and achieve their own goals, thereby being able to work towards helping themselves and others to maximize the quality of their lives.

Moser (1989) defined empowerment is the capacity of women to increase their own self-reliance and internal strength. This is identified as the right to determine choices in life and to influence the direction of change through the ability to gain control over material and non-material resources. In the words of Clutterbuck and Stuart (1992), we need not 'empower women' but 'power women'.

Dubhushi (1997) considered empowerment as exercising control over ones lives, firstly, on resources of financial, physical and human and secondly, on beliefs, values and attitudes.

The Social Work Dictionary (Barker, 1991), defines empowerment as "the process of helping a group or community to achieve political influence or relevant legal authority".

According to Zippy (1995), empowerment represents "a means for accomplishing community development tasks and can be conceptualized as involving two key elements giving community members the authority to make decisions and choices and facilitating the development of the knowledge and resources necessary to exercise these choices".

J.K. Pillai (1995), discussed "Empowerment is an active, multidimensional process which enables women to realize their full identity and powers in all spheres of life". Power is not commodity to be transacted; nor can it be given away as aims. "Power has to be acquired and once acquired, it needs to be once acquired, its needs to be exercised, sustained and preserved".

According to Bandura (1986), "Empowerment is the process through which individuals gain efficacy, defined as the degree to which an individual perceives that he or she controls his or her environment".

Chandra Shanti Kohli (1997) defined empowerment in its simplest form means "the manifestation of redistribution of power that challenges patriarchal ideology and the male dominance".

People from different fields define empowerment in different ways. Policy-makers, development planners, activists, researchers and aid agencies have tried to define it by emphasizing on different aspects. According to M. Hapke Holly, empowerment is "access to and control over productive resources, knowledge and awareness of one's self and society personal needs, health issues, legal rights, technological innovations and the availability of social and economic resources, how to take advantage of them, self-image, that is, realization of one's capabilities and the potential and confidence to take action in one's life are the components of empowerment".

Gitte Sorensen and Helle Poulsen defined empowerment "as gaining autonomy and control over one's life. The empowered becomes agents of their own development, are able to exercise choices, set their own agenda, and are capable of challenging and changing their subordinate position in society".

Divya Pandey defines it "as a process of building capacities and confidence for taking decisions about one's own life at an individual and collective level and gaining control over productive resources that are developed and built. The empowerment process is facilitated by creating awareness about one's rights and responsibilities and socio-economic, educational and political opportunities, by developing skills for utilizing productive resources and by involving oneself in collective activities and community life".

M.C. Whirter defines empowerment as "the process by which peoples, organization or groups who are powerless:

- become aware of the power dynamics at work, in their life context,
- develop the skills and capacity for gaining some reasonable control over their level,
- exercise this control without infringing upon the rights of others, and
- Support the empowerment of others in the community."

Feminist interpretations of power led to a still broader understanding of empowerment. Since they go beyond formal and institutional definitions of power and incorporate the idea of 'the personal as political'. From a feminist perspective, 'power over' entails understanding the dynamics of operation and internalized operation. Empowerment if thus more than participation in decision-making; it must also includes process that lead people to perceive themselves as able and entitled to make decisions. The feminist understanding of empowerment includes 'power to' and 'power from within' (Jo Rowland, 1997).

"Empowerment in the context of gender and development is most usefully defined as a process rather than end product; it is dynamic and changing and varies widely according to circumstances. Empowerment process will take a form which arises out of a particular cultural, ethnic, historical, economical, geographical, political and social location; out of an individuals place in the life cycle, specific life experience and out of the interaction of all the above with gender relations prevailing in society" (Jo Rowland, 1997).

Empowerment is a multi-dimensional process which enables an individual to realize his or her full ideality and identity of his full potentiality. This is closely related to control over the resources, enabling a person to exercise his independent views. Several researchers have tried to capture the meaning of the word empowerment. In simple terms, empowerment is the process to give or delegate power or authority to, or to give ability to, or enable or permit the target. It consist of greater access to knowledge and resources, greater autonomy in decision-making to enable them to have greater ability to plan their lives, or have greater control over the circumstances that influence their lives and free them from shackles imposed on them by custom, belief and practice. In general, development with justice is expected to generate the forces that lead to empowerment of various sections of population in a country and to uplift their living standard.

The terminology of empowerment has arisen from the theoretical debates as well as practical debates especially from the experience of women working at the grass-root level in many parts of the world. In 1990s when terms like 'participation', 'consultation' and 'partnership' began to enter the development thinking importance given by development agencies was shifted to enabling approach, that is, enabling people to identify and express their needs and priorities. It is in this context the notion of empowerment has arisen (Jo Rowland, 1997).

Empowerment is an active process. Power is not a commodity to be transacted. Power cannot be given away as alms. Power has to be acquired. Once acquired, it needs to be exercised, sustained and preserved. Women have to empower themselves.

While discussing empowerment Jo Rowland (1997) has identified four different forms of powers:

- Power over—control or influence over others which is an instrumentation of domination;
- Power to—generative or productive power which creates new possibilities and actions without domination;
- Power with—a sense of the whole being greater than the sum of the individuals, especially when a group tackles problems together;
- Power from within—the spiritual strength and uniqueness that resides in each one of us and make us truly human. Its basis is self-acceptance and self-respect which extend, in turn, respect for and acceptance of others as equals.

Though the interpretation 'power to' and 'power with' empowerment is concerned with the process by which people become aware of their interest and how those relates to the interests of others but also participates in decision-making and influence such decisions (Jo Rowland, 1997).

There are several kinds of relational power (Jo Rowland, 1998). These include:

Power over—controlling power,
Power to—generate new possibilities without domination,
Power with—collective power, power created by group process, and
Power from within—spiritual strength that inspires and energizes others.

"Power over" is especially relevant here, as it refers to those who have access to formal decision-making process. Real change may not be possible unless we address power inequalities between marginalized individuals and groups at the grassroots and those who make policy and aid decisions. The other kinds of power—power to, power with and power from within—may be instrumental in attaining greater power over.

The process of empowerment involves reformation changes in access to resources, but also an understanding of one's rights and entitlement and the conscientization that "gender roles can be changed and gender equality is possible" (Longwe, as reported in the centre for Development and Population Activities, 1996).

Any attempt to improve their status should start with empowerment. It is the process through which individuals gain efficacy, defined as the degree to which an individual perceives that he or she controls his or her environment (Bandura, 1986).

According to Hapke (1992), empowerment should include:

- Access to and control over productive resources,
- Knowledge and awareness of one's self and society, and of personal needs, health issues, legal rights, technological innovations and availability of social and economic resources and how to take advantage of them,
- Self-image, and
- Autonomy.

Chandra defined, "Empowerment of women in its simplest form means the manifestation of redistribution of power that challenges patriarchal ideology and the male dominance. It is both a process and the result of the process".

The following definitions and descriptions of the term empowerment are useful. According to Fawcett (1984), "community empowerment is the process of increasing control by groups over consequences that are important to their members and to others in the broader community".

Rappaport (1987) describes empowerment as "a psychological sense of personal control or influence and a concern with actual social influence, political power and legal rights. It is multi-level construct applicable to individual citizens as well as to organizations and neighbourhoods; it suggests the study of people in context".

In summary, empowerment is the "manifestation of social power at individual, organizational and community-levels of analysis" (Speer and Hughey, 1995).

Most women across the globe rely on the informal work sector for an income. If women were empowered to do more and be more, the possibility for economic growth becomes apparent. Eliminating a significant part of a nation's work force on the sole basis of gender can have detrimental effects on the economy of that nation. In addition, female participation in counsels, groups, and businesses is seen to increase efficiency. For a general idea on how an empowered woman can impact a situation monetarily, a study found that of fortune 500 companies, "those with more women board directors had significantly higher financial returns, including 53 percent higher returns on equity, 24 percent higher returns on sales and 67 percent higher returns on invested capital (OECD, 2008)." This study shows the impact women can have on the overall economic benefits of a company. If implemented on a global scale, the inclusion of women in the formal workforce (like a fortune 500 company) can increase the economic output of a nation.

Many of the barriers to women empowerment and equity lie ingrained into the cultures of certain nations and societies. Many women feel these pressures, while others have become accustomed to being treated inferior to men. Even if men, legislators, NGOs, etc. are aware of the benefits women empowerment and participation can have, many are scared of disrupting the *status quo* and continue to let societal get in the way of development.

Process

The process which enables individuals/groups to fully access personal/collective power, authority and influence, and to employ that strength when engaging with other people, institutions or society. In other words, "Empowerment is not giving people power, people already have plenty of power, in the wealth of their knowledge and motivation, to do their jobs magnificently. We define empowerment as letting this power out (Blanchard, K.)." It encourages people to gain the skills and knowledge that will allow them to overcome obstacles in life or work environment and ultimately, help them develop within themselves or in the society.

To empower a female "...sounds as though we are dismissing or ignoring males, but the truth is, both genders desperately need to be equally empowered." (Dr. Asa Don Brown) Empowerment occurs through improvement of conditions, standards, events, and a global perspective of life.

Workplace

According to Thomas A. Potterfield, many organizational theorists and practitioners regard employee empowerment as one of the most important and popular management concepts of our time. Ciulla discusses an inverse case: that of bogus empowerment.

In Management

Ken Blanchard, John P. Carlos, and Alan Randolph, illustrate three keys that organizations can use to open the knowledge, experience, and motivation power that people already have. The three keys that managers must use to empower their employees are:

1. Share information with everyone,
2. Create autonomy through boundaries, and
3. Replace the old hierarchy with self-managed teams.

According to Stewart, in her book *Empowering People* she describes that in order to guarantee a successful work environment, managers need to exercise the "right kind of authority" (p. 6). To summarize, "empowerment is simply the effective use of a manager's authority", and subsequently, it is a productive way to maximize all-around work efficiency. These keys are hard to put into place and it is a journey to achieve empowerment in a workplace. It is important to train employees and make sure they have trust in what empowerment will bring to a company.

Economics

In economic development, the empowerment approach focuses

on mobilizing the self-help efforts of the poor, rather than providing them with social welfare. Economic empowerment is also the empowering of previously disadvantaged sections of the population, for example, in many previously colonized African countries.

NATIONAL MISSION FOR EMPOWERMENT OF WOMEN

The National Mission for Empowerment of Women (NMEW) was launched by the Government of India on International Women's Day in 2010 with the aim to strengthen overall processes that promote all-round development of women. It has the mandate to strengthen the inter-sector convergence; facilitate the process of coordinating all the women's welfare and socio-economic development programmes across ministries and departments. The Mission aims to provide a single window service for all programmes run by the Government for Women under aegis of various Central Ministries.

In light with its mandate, the Mission has been named Mission Poorna Shakti, implying a vision for holistic empowerment of women. The National Resource Centre for Women has been set-up which functions as a national convergence centre for all schemes and programmes for women. It acts as a central repository of knowledge, information, research and data on all gender-related issues and is the main body servicing the National and State Mission Authority.

Mission Statement

NMEW will achieve gender equality, and gender justice and holistic development of women through inter-sectoral convergence of program relating to women, forging synergy between various stakeholders and creating an enabling environment conducive to social change.

Women constitute roughly half of the population. But, the condition of women when we see through the prism of gender equality and gender parity looks terribly miserable. In all walks of life women are lagging behind. We see under representation of them in prominent fields and remain a marginal force in politics, industry and administration. The condition of poor women is pathetic. Many of them suffer poverty, discrimination and untold violence. Almost all women without any exception are feeling weak and powerless in one-way or another. Empowerment is the need of the time. Various strategies used to ameliorate the condition of women like "women's welfare", upliftment development or awareness rising have not produced the desired results.

Women constitute 48% of the total population of India as per census and constituting about half of the world's population, are the most important human resources central to the development of any race, culture or civilization. In Gandhi's view 'one step for a woman ten steps for nation'. As such the role and participation of woman in society cannot be ignored. Like men, women are also found to be working in various fields be from shop assistants to managers from clerks, typists, telephone operators, receptionists, to those who bold highest responsible posts in public sector, from primary school teachers to university professors, from private medical practitioners to hospital superintendents. They are in a variety of occupation becomes their motivational factors are they come from varied socio-economic and cultural backgrounds.

The word empowerment is widely used in relation to women. Very often it is used as a substitute for women's welfare, development of women, upliftment of women, participation and conscientisation of women. But, the concept of empowerment is not synonymous to these words. It is something of a more and broader concept.

Empowerment of women seems to be the true option available before us to improve the condition of women and to establish gender equality and justice. The term women's empowerment has come to be associated with women's struggle for social justice and equality. In every society there are powerful and powerless groups. Power is exercised in social, economic and political relations between individuals and groups. In our modern patriarchic society, women have become powerless under the oppression of men. Unless they are empowered we cannot realize development.

Empowerment of women also means extension of choices in personal life regarding education, employment, marriage, etc. Increasing choices in women's life depends on the support give by family members, institutional agencies and community.

U.K. Anand (2001) state that for empowerment of women in every field the economic independence is of paramount importance. Empowerment of women means, thereby adequate access to resources, power and decision-making is a pre-requisite towards gender justice. Women and economic empowerment has been recognized that women can and are contributing to national development. Women's participation in nation development is not merely a question of providing some special concession to them. Women's collective action on issues of relevance for their empowerment is the key factor which women's movement as a whole has to be organized and directed.

Nobel Prize winner Prof. Amartya Sen, emphasized that unless women are empowered, issues like health, literacy and population will remain unsolved problems of the developing countries in this part of the sub-continent. Empowerment of women is attempted to address two important issues:

- Reducing gender inequalities (discrimination), and
- Building equality in nation's development (enhancing women's participation).

Gender and Human Rights

World-over, women are denied their human rights. Gender differentiation is about inequality and about power relations between men and women. Half the world's population is subordinate to the other half, in thousands of different ways, because of the sex they are born with. Despite international human rights law which guarantees all people equal rights irrespective of sex, race, caste, and so on, women are denied equal rights with men to land, property to mobility, to education, to employment opportunities, to shelter, to food, to worship and over the lives of their children.

Women are denied the right even to marriage, control and care for health of their own bodies and their reproductive function. In many cultures women's bodies are ritually maimed and mutilated and women are routinely beaten and even murdered in the name of cultural tradition in spite of the fact that international human rights law prohibits cultural practices which are damaging to women. Violence against women is an abuse of human rights.

Women's Multiple Role

Women are usually the carriers, the nurtures, the educators, the source of stability and increasingly they are major cash contributors. For the most part, women meet their responsibilities to their children, their men and orders of infirm relatives with generosity, self-sacrifice and unstinting labour. Few deny that women in every society carry out multiple roles both within the family and outside. Women have responsibilities which can be roughly categorized as: Reproductive (child bearing and rearing), Caring for their family members, the ill, the infirm and the elderly and Household domestic work including growing, buying and preparing food.

Along with these is what is called productive work: agriculture and earning an income in the full range of trades and professions. Recent researches have identified other areas of responsibility:

Community management—it includes all activities in the public sphere, from organizing festivals and caring for the sick, to lobbying authorities for services, forming a trade union, holding political office, etc.

Environmental management—it includes food producers, fuel and water gatherers, and natural resource managers.

But, women are frequently excluded from development planning and environmental conservation decision-making, in spite of the fact that they are capable of carrying out multiple roles, mainly because of biological differences and gender discriminated roles. People are born female or male, but learn to be girls and boys who grow into women and men. They are taught the appropriate behaviour and attitudes, roles and activities and how they should relate to their people. This learned behaviour is what makes up gender identity and determining gender roles causing inequality to women. Women, who constitute almost half of the world's population, are disadvantaged in many ways. They constitute the majority of the illiterates.

The underemployed (low paid) and the most economically and socially disadvantaged groups. Poorer women worked longer hours than men, usually starting at 5 or 6 in the morning and ending at 10 or 12 in the night. This is because women bore the double burden of productive and non-productive activities. Their primary role as caretaker of the family did not change regardless of their wage earning status. Despite this double work a day, women were considered economically unproductive (Sangeetha Purushotham, 1988)

Men took away money from women without asking, when a woman acquired assets or applied for credit allotted specifically for women. It was often in name only. But, the decision on how to use the resource was made by her husband. Resources given to her by her family during the time of marriage or even afterwards were rarely regarded as belonging to her and usually went to her husband or family (Sangeetha Purushotham, 1988)

In order to save women against all those gender discriminated inequalities, she should be empowered to have control over her possessions, to be self-reliant and capable of taking self-decisions for their own good and also for building equality in families.

Human rights for women is the collective right of a woman to be seen and accepted as a person with the capacity to decide or act on her own behalf and to have equal access to resources and equitable social, economic and political support to develop her full potential, exercise her right as a full human being and to support the development of others (Asia Pacific Forum on Women, 1990). An essential first step to building equality is to remove gender-based discrimination against women.

Extensive discrimination against women violates the principles of equality of rights and respect for human dignity, is an obstacle to the participation of women, on equal terms with men, in the political, social, economic and cultural life of their countries, hampers the growth and prosperity of society and the family and make more difficult the full development of the potentialities of women in the service of their countries and of humanity.

In every society, women profoundly influence the lives and well being of their families and their surrounding communities. In most cultures, women are the primary managers of natural resources including food, shelter and consumption of goods within the family unit. Increasingly, they also hold jobs and have careers in the formal economy. Women's activities and responsibilities place them in a unique position to improve human well-being and preserve and maintain the environment. It is the future management of these three factors: the quality of human life, the global economy and the environment that will determine whether we have a sustainable future.

Even though, women have a pivotal role in the world's future, their needs, their work and their voices are often ignored. They do not have equal access to education, healthcare, employment, land, credit, technology or political power and they are not equal participants in programmes and decisions that affect their future.

Women around the world, in the context of cultural traditions of violence against women, such as bride burning in India and female circumcision in some African countries, where discriminatory laws have been stricken from the books, discriminatory practices may still prevent women participating fully in political and economic life. Even in the most advanced countries, women's perspectives rarely predominate in political or economic decision-making. Women make up half of the world's population, but hold less than 5% of the world's heads of states positions, chief executive positions of major corporations and top positions in international organizations.

This situation is an injustice in itself, but it also has larger social and economic implications. Failure to provide equal opportunities for women to pursue education and economic self-sufficiency has meant that disproportionate number of women were poor. Without education, they are stuck in low paying, low status jobs if they are able to work at all. These social barriers exclusion low status and poverty are also barriers to a sustainable environment.

Development programmes designed to raise the standard of living for communities while also managing the area's natural resources—make an important contribution to sustainable development. But, few women have held decision-making positions in development and environmental management programmes. On an average, less than 5% of the management-level staff of development agencies is women (World Resources, 1994-95).

Thus, development policies have been made by men and reflect their priorities. Economic development policies in many countries have focused on the production of goods for export: cash crops, primary commodities and industrial goods—activities controlled mainly by men.

Agricultural extension services have been staffed almost entirely by men and offered to men, even though, approximately half the world's food is grown by women, and in some cultures it is not acceptable for women to meet a man to receive instruction in farming techniques.

To promote a sustainable future, development projects need to address inequalities and focus on creating an environment in which men and women can prosper together. This means creating programmes that increase women's control over income and household resources, improve their productivity, establish their legal and social rights and increase the social and economic choices they are able to make.

Any society wishing to make material and spiritual progress must assure that women are fully integrated into its productive, educational, cultural and political activities. Women must be active participants in decision-making at all levels.

At present, there are various social and cultural barriers to women's participation in the nation's development. Early marriage, high bride price, domestic and rural drudgery, discriminatory family treatment and old age insecurity are some of the social injustices that afflict womanhood. Involving women is essential for national development and for this to take place it is indispensable to change attitudes of the population, to strengthen and enforce the laws and to have the new social consciousness of the principle of equality between the sexes and above all the empowerment of women.

The reason for such state of powerlessness issues—

- Women's dependence on men.
- Retrograde social values.
- Lack of education and skills.
- Lack of awareness about their rights.
- Lack of gender solidarity for collective action.
- Lack of opportunities for women.
- Gender bias.

These are all the result of patriarchal society, which favors and justifies the domination of men over women.

Female empowerment approach stresses the capacity of women to increase their self-reliance and internal strength. It aims at restructuring of gender relations within both family and in society at large, and it is society's recognition of women's equality with men. Further, it is an accepted fact that fruits of development are most equitably distributed and enjoyed equitably when development strategies are women centred.

Karl (1995) opines that empowerment of women involves four interrelated and mutually reinforcing components:

- Collective awareness and capacity building and skills development,
- Participation and greater control,

- Decision-making power, and
- Action to bring about gender equality.

Thus, it implies control over decision-making process, both at personal and cooperative, control over income and expenditure, and acquisition and exercise of knowledge. It has four dimensions: economic, social, political and psychological.

Empowerment of people requires action on:

- Investing in education and health of the people so that they can take advantage of market opportunities,
- Ensuring an enabling environment that gives everyone access to credit and productive assets so that playing fields of lives are more even, and
- Empowering both women and men so that they can compete on equal footing. It gives people of a community the ability and opportunity to take part in decision-making process with regard to socio-economic and political issues affecting their existence.

Empowerment of the deprived beings with their ability to voice their opinion through the process of consensuses politics and dialogue, backed up by access to education, information, organization, employment and credit (Sengupta, 1998).

Women's empowerment has recently gained considerable importance as an area of policy intervention in most part of the world. Government has recognized the benefits of empowerment which can be achieved through effective participation of women. It is a term often used in development work, but rarely defined. In a conventional sense, empowerment brings people who are outside the decision-making process into it (Rowlands, 1997). It puts a strong emphasis on participation in political structures and formal decision-making and on the ability to obtain an income that enables participation in economic decision-making.

When viewed from the point of 'power to' and 'power with', empowerment is concerned with process by which people become aware of their own interests and how those relate to interests of others in order both to participate from a position of greater strength in decision-making and actually to influence such decision. From a feminist perspective, empowerment is more than participation in decision-making. It also includes the process that leads people to perceive themselves as able and entitled to make decision. It involves giving scope to full range of human abilities and potential. Empowerment must involve undoing negative social construction, so that come to see themselves as having the capacity and right to act and influence decisions (Rowlands, 1997).

While empowerment literally means 'to invest with power' in the context of women's empowerment, the term has come to denote women's increased control over their own lives, bodies and environment. Women empowerment is a social process which neutralizes the oppression against the society and establishes the equity. Emphasis is placed on women's decision-making roles, their economic self-reliance, their legal rights to equal treatment, inheritance and protection against all forms of discrimination (Germaine and Kyte, 1995; United Nations, 1995) in addition to the elimination of barriers to their access of resources such as education and information.

By empowerment we mean a wide range of activities from individual self-assertion to collective resistance, protest and mobilization that challenge the basic power relations. The outcome of empowerment would be a distribution of power between classes, castes, races, ethnic groups or genders. As such, the main goal of empowerment is to challenge subordination and subjugation and to transform the structures, systems and institutions, which have supported inequality (Srilatha Batliwala, 1993).

The process of empowerment must really begin in mind with a new consciousness that question the existing inequality situations supported by the prevailing structure and systems of the society. Thus, the process is one where women find a time and space of their own and begin to reexamine their lives collectively. This will enable them to look and act towards their old problem in a different way to analyze their environment and situations, to recognize their strength, alter their self image, access to new information and knowledge, to acquire new skills and finally to initiate action aimed at gaining control over resources of various kinds.

Empowerment is not merely a change of mind set, but a visible demonstration of that change which the world is forced to acknowledge, respond to and accommodates as best it may (Srilatha Batliwala, 1993). With their growing collective strength, women begin to asset their right to control resources and participate equally in decision-making within the family, community and village. As poor women begin to identified and act on the problem and issues through a process of collective strength, the begin the struggle to gain access and control of resources like land, employment, food, water, housing, bank and credit system, health and child care, natural resources and legal system. This is where the external agencies supporting the empowerment process has to make its own choices and strategic decisions.

It is difficult to measure empowerment. There is no single method for measuring it. It should be understood and defined through indicators. Indicators of empowerment should encompass personal, social, economic and political change. Empowerment is a term generally used to describe a process by which powerless people, conscious of their own situation and organize collectively to gain greater access to public service or to the benefits of economic growth.

The global conference on women's empowerment 1988 highlighted empowerment as the surest way of making women partners in development. Empowerment is an active process enabling women to realize their full identity and power in all spheres of life.

As far as women's empowerment is concerned M. Hake Holly says, "it is restructuring of gender relations within both family and society at large and it is society's recognition of women's equality with men in terms of their worth to society as independent person".

According to The National Policy of Education, Government of India (1986) women become empowered through collective reflection and decision-making. Its parameters are building a positive self image and self-confidence, developing the ability to think critically, building up group cohesion and fostering decision-making and action, ensuring equal participation in the process of bringing about social change, encouraging group action in order to bring about change in the society, providing the wherewithal for economic independence".

Naila Kabir defines women's empowerment as "a process whereby women become able to organize themselves to increase their own self-reliance, to assert their independent right, to make choices and to control resources which will assist in challenging and eliminating their own subordination".

Caroline Moser's definition focuses on individual empowerment and it considers control of resources as the main means to achieve empowerment. According to her, "empowerment is the capability of women to increase their own self-reliance and internal strength. This is identified as the right to determine the choices in life and to influence the direction of change, through the ability to gain control over material and non-material resources".

The word "Empowerment" has been given currency by UN agencies during recent years. It is beginning to get known in India also. Empowerment is basically concerned with recognition of women's individuality. The issue of empowerment has arisen precisely because in a man-dominated world women have been denied equality of status and opportunities for centuries. It is an integral part of the development process which ought to integrate economic, political, legal and cultural aspects. Such a process of necessity involved the democratization process.

The concept of empowerment of an individual or a social group pre supposes that a state of social, oppression exists which has disempowered those in the group, by denying them opportunities or resources and by subjecting them to an ideology and a set of social practices which has defined them as inferior humans, thus lowering their self-esteem. As general goal, empowerment has been described as a political and a material process, which increases individual and group power, self-reliance and strength (Nigel and Werner, 2002).

Constitutions and legislations do not always bring about social change. What is needed is a more holistic perception of the development process and the conditions of the operations of the democratic system. Further, there cannot possibly be, from the women's point of view, a socio-political-economic programme for women alone; the need would arise to develop a comprehensive programme for the society as a whole from women's perspectives. This obviously relates to gender equality as a human development objective.

Today's girl child is tomorrow's woman. If tomorrow's women is to become an equal partner with man, there is a great need to accord the girl child her rightful share of dignity and opportunity today. Her physical, mental, emotional, intellectual and spiritual development will determine the quality of life of her family and generation to come. Although, the girl child has a natural biological advantage over the boy, yet in India, social disadvantage outweighs the genetic advantage of girls. As per 2001 Census, there are 495.7 million women.

There is a strong gender has in Indian society which idolizes son. As a result of customs, rituals and traditional practices girls are denied optimal opportunities for growth and development and treated as "lower child" (Amin, 2001). Girl child in India is subjected to 'inequality', 'disparity' and 'neglect'. Gender based inequalities permeate the very fabric of the social and cultural environment and the value system. Equality of opportunities between the sexes is enshrined in the Indian Constitution but it is still a distant dream and not a reality as far as women are concerned.

The process of women's empowerment is multi-dimensional. It enables women to realize their full potential and empower them in all spheres of life. Empowerment as a concept, therefore, encompasses their political empowerment, economic independence and social upliftment (Kant, 2001). The concept of empowerment of mother and girl child as a goal of development projects and programme has been gaining wider acceptance.

A salient feature of the term empowerment is that it contains within the word 'POWER'. This power operates in various fields of life as economic, social, political, religious, educational, etc. successive and continual denial of two of the most important sources of power, that is, education and economic independence has resulted in large scale powerlessness among women. Global Conference on Women's Empowerment highlighted the empowerment as the surest way of making them as partners in development (Chatterji, 1988).

Empowerment, therefore, is a process which enables women to realize their identity and power in all aspects of life. It enables to have more access to knowledge and resources, greater autonomy in decision-making, greater ability to plan their time, free from clutches of irrelevant customs, traditional and practices. "Empowerment and education are the keys to building self-esteem necessary for girls to understand and assert their rights and to act on behalf of their own advancement". Empowerment is power that stems from knowledge and skill acquired, action taken and their inner strength gained from educational experience (Nagarajan, 1998).

Empowerment is not a new concept. Every society has local terms for autonomy, self-direction, self-confidence, self-worth. What is new is the attempt to measure empowerment in a systematic way.

Empowerment as a concept is the result of the process which enables an individual to know about herself/himself, what she/he wants, express it, try to get it and get what she/he wants, have confidence, awareness, mobility, choices, control over resources and decision-making power. The process, which enables an individual to gain the above qualities, is called empowerment.

The process of gaining control over the resources ideology and self, which determine power, can be called empowerment. When we apply this definition of power empowerment of women, it is clear that women do not have power (are powerless) since they do not have control over resources. Even if they have, it is only to some extent over some resources. This power is limited by patriarchal norms, customs, traditions and social values imposed on them. In the family man is considered as breadwinner, physical and financial assets are in his name and control, naturally power is in his hands. Women being deprived of access to and control over resources are denied of power.

Even in the case of community, public property, resources, institutions and political power is concentrated in the hands of men. Women are kept out of this domain. In this context, women should have power by gaining control over the resources ideology and self. Empowerment of women is of great need. But, empowerment is not limited to power. It is a larger and broader concept with vaster and different dimensions.

Everyone needs empowerment at all levels. It involves gaining confidence to voice opinion, access to information, exposure to new ideas and experiences, taking responsibility to make decisions and taking risks. Empowerment can be achieved through training, networking, developing positive role models and facilitating the process of empowerment. There arises a question why there is a need for empowering the people? It is to identify the real and the appropriate needs, encourage commitment, ensure sustainability and personal development, create self-esteem and enable them to share power (District Primary Education Programme, Newsletter, November, 1998).

The way of defining empowerment, choosing indicators of empowerment and objective of empowerment depends on whether the area of empowerment covered is individual growth or social and political change or both. Type of empowerment, time period, and target group whose empowerments we are discussing are more important in the process of empowerment. On whatever way empowerment is defined and understood it has limitations since it is related to states of mind and is qualitative in nature. Besides, elements of empowerment like knowledge, self-respect, confidence and awareness are cultural specific and they vary among localities and by socio-economic groups. So, it is not possible to impose all indicators, meanings, to one individual or one indicators or one meaning to all individuals (Guide to Gender Sensitive Indicators, CIDA, Canada, 1996).

The concept of empowerment is frequently associated with women in today's world. Empowerment of women has become a catchy slogan among different social groups. The government, the political parties, women's organization, etc. are involved in the so called empowerment process. This is quite understandable given the social economic status of women in the present day world. Empowerment is a very broad concept and it is applicable to different areas of social concern. Empowerment is a desired goal in areas like management and labour unions, health care and ecology, education and literary, etc. Women development has become one important area of concern.

The concept of empowerment has fairly long history. It emerged and became prominent during the civil rights movement of the block Americans in the 1960's. Dissatisfied with the scope and pace of social reforms the block leaders called for empowering themselves. The black leaders thought instead of begging for denied rights it is better to empower themselves. This shift in the direction of civil rights movement in America was responsible for the birth of concept empowerment. Empowerment became popular among women's activities only during the mid-1970's. The women activities after many prolonged struggles finally came to the conclusion, which is similar to that of black leaders. The conclusion was to take power instead of demanding for it. As a result of this empowerment of women has become an important process throughout the world today.

The empowerment process is expected to change the distribution of power both in interpersonal relations and in social institutions throughout the society. Women as a daughter, student, and wife and as a professional are expected to play the subordinate role. The existing social institution in the society also prescribes a subordinate and dependent position for women. This is because the social values which structure the gender relations are based on notions like women are physically and mentally weaker than the men. They are suitable for certain specific roles like mother therefore the empowerment process advocates initiatives by women themselves to change the existing gender based discrimination. The empowerment in its application has different shades of meaning. It advocates self-reliance rather than dependency on others. For acquiring power it links action to needs and encourages action for collective change. The empowerment is not nearly concerned with personal development of women alone. It endeavors to analyze such areas like human rights and social justice.

The concept of empowerment is applicable to women as a whole but in different ways and dimensions to different groups according to the country, class, caste and the society they belong to. "The use of the concept of empowerment has greater relevance and application to 'third world' countries which are characterized by high levels of poverty, feminization of poverty, low female literacy, invisibility of women, strong patriarchal and community values (N.K. Banerjee, 1995).

The term empowerment of women is as important popular concept among political spectrum. Empowerment through the expansion of the civil, political and social rights of citizenship is a laborious and unexciting process. Empowerment is only effective answer to oppression, exploitation, injustice, and other melodies of society. The idea of empowerment contains exciting possibilities. Empowerment is a wide term with no specific meaning. The term is very vague is more a context driven rather than theory driven.

Empowerment is about social transformation. It is about the people rather than politicians. It is about power, although the concept of power contained in it is generally left unspecified. Empowerment is both a means to an end in itself. The focus on empowerment has given a new emphasis to the building of economic and social capabilities among individuals, classes and communities. It is theory of social change in particular, a change from a hierarchical to and egalitarian type of society. It is based on democratic society, which is based on recognition of equal rights to all individuals in its place. Empowerment appears to be an alternative path for dismantling the old structure and putting new one in this place. Empowerment is to change the society through re-arrangement of the power. So, there is a need for empowerment through civic, political and social rights of citizens.

The 'Empowerment Strategy' in the Beijing Conference report states, "If women are to be empowered, it is necessary to provide and expending networking of support service so that they are freed from some of their gender related shackles. If women are to be economically empowered, they are to be provided with additional channels of credit training, employment, greater visibility, management skills and social security. If women to be politically empowered, the immediate imperative is to resort to different forms of affirmative action so that their voices are heard. If women are to be persons in their own right, they must be in control of their own bodies and suitably empowered.

The empowerment process in the First world is different from that of the Third world. It is more strategical, that is, changing patriarchal norms, gender division of labour, gaining equality and changing the attitudes of society towards women in the First world. While in the Third world it is more practical to meet the basic needs, increase in income, educating and give training in skill development to meet along with strategic gender needs. Meeting both practical needs and strategic interests are necessary to empower women. Women are the main caretakers in the families below the poverty line.

Hence, practical needs of these women related to daily life—food, housing, income, health-care and welfare benefits ought to be meets. But, mere meeting practical needs do not empower women unless strategic interests are fulfilled. Strategic interests are long-term and common to almost all women. They are related to improving women's position. They include action to increase women's knowledge and skills, give them legal protection and provide equal opportunities and equal participation in decision-making and greater access to resources, etc. Strategic interests transform gender relations and empower women.

Women empowerment implies individual as well as collective empowerment. Individual empowerment is building positive self-image and self-confidence, developing the ability to think critically, cultivating decision-making power, etc. "Collective empowerment means enabling women collectively to take control of their own lives, to set their own agenda, to organize to help each other and make demands on the state for support and on society itself for change" (Kate Young, 1993).

Collective empowerment is joining of women together to get access to public resources, to fight against injustices done to them and to amend the existing laws, policies and programmes, which are unfavourable to women.

The concept of women empowerment is the outcome of several important critiques and debates generated by the women's movement throughout the world, particularly by the Third World feminists. Its source can be traced from the interaction between feminism and the concept of "Popular Education" developed in Latin America in the 1970's (Walters, 1991). The concept of women empowerment has its roots throughout the world in women's movement.

Women empowerment is based on the premise that it is an enabling condition for reproductive rights. The nature and priorities of the women's empowerment process are shaped by the historical, political, social and economic conditions. The concept of women empowerment appears to be the outcome of several important critiques and debates generated by the women's movement throughout the world. The source of women empowerment can be traced to the interaction between feminism and the concept of popular education. Gender subordination and the social construction of gender was a prior in feminist analysis and popular education.

It is difficult to measure empowerment. There is no single method for measuring it. It should be understood and defined through indicators. Indicators of empowerment should encompass personal, social, economic and political change. Empowerment is a term generally used to describe a process by which powerless people become conscious of their own situation and organize collectively to gain greater access to public service or to the benefits of economic growth.

To promote women empowerment the world conference has provided a broad-based activity schedule to the national, regional and global agencies, in which participation of women in the decision-making process could be enhanced many fold and the progress attained in a much shorter-time span. The process of empowerment is helping in identifying areas to be targeted, planning, strategies for acting and in analysis of action and outcomes. Empowerment is not a process which is horizontal or vertical. It is a process which goes round in a circle. Here, the beginning ends in a change and the change leads to another beginning. No one magic formula or fail-safe design can exist for empowerment. It has to be tailor made to suit the clients.

Actually, the situation of women has changed completely 1990 onwards. At the beginning of the 1970s women were a blind spot in both development aid and the debate on it. The promotion of women is now established in all State Institutions and Non-Governmental Organizations. Gender training is to sensitive development workers to take a gender specific approach in analyzing development processes, carrying out statistical surveys and planning and evaluating activities.

Those women who in the 1970s criticized development policy and its actors for being one-eyed must now see themselves as line-promoters and idea-providers. All the terms they used have been adopted in official usage. The image of the women has changed from being a Cinderella—like, hard-done—by person, the poor soul, the victim, to a dynamic, reliable actor with apparently inexhaustible reserves of energy and creativity to bring to bear in a development process that has got stuck.

The concept of empowerment has replaced the old "integration in development" approach in the promotion of women, that is, the women's approach (Gender and Development). This calls for the inclusion of men, taking a close look at the gender relationship and changing it into the long-run. The empowerment concept makes clear the political and economic gap between men and women, it aims at a redistribution of social power and control of resources in favour of women based on a development strategy, which is no longer, oriented on growth, the world market and military power.

The concept has had seemingly record acceptance in the executive suites and programmes of the Governments while at the same time its substances has been drastically diluted. Taken on board book-line-and-sinker by official policy, its politically critical teeth—namely, posing the power question—have been extracted. It now has no bite critical or development and social policy. It just stands modestly and harmlessly for every strengthening and participation of women.

Empowerment of women is gaining added significance in the Indian context owing to their greater participation in developmental activities. Women empowerment cannot be rigidly defined, particularly, in a situation like ours, where there exits a lot of difference among women in different sectors such as rural *vs.* urban women; women in organized sector *vs.* women in unorganized sector or informal sector; women in Government/public sector *vs.* those in private sector; educated women *vs.* uneducated women, both in rural and urban sectors; and women belonging to lower-level income group *vs.* those belonging to higher income group. Above all, one finds glaring differences between women belonging to upper castes, class and religion those belonging to lower classes. All these differences cited above are crucial factors to reckon with before anyone attempts to define the concept empowerment of women and then analyzing the determinants of the same.

In other words, empowerment is influenced by a host of socio-economic, political and cultural factors. In the words of Bharadwaj, empowerment of women is basically determined by their socio-economic status. Socio-economic status would therefore be a ranking of an individual by the society he/she lives in, in terms of his/her material belongings and cultural possessions along with the degree of respect, power and influence he/she wields. (Bharatwaj, 1980).

We can deal with empowerment in two ways. One is empowerment in general in relation to the poor or those who are powerless. Second, one is the empowerment of women. "For the first time Paulo Frier mentioned the term empowerment in his theories by using 'conscientization' a process by which poor could challenge the structure of power and take control of their lives. But, he ignored gender as one of the determinants of power. Feminist by including gender aspect to empowerment expand the Freirian's empowerment analysis" (Srilatha Batliwala, 1995).

The process of challenging existing power relations, and of gaining greater control over the sources of power, may be termed empowerment. There is some degree of anxiety about whether women empowerment leads to the disempowerment of men. It is obvious that poor men are almost as powerless as poor women in terms of access to and control over resources. This is exactly why most poor men tend to support women empowerment processes that enable women to bring much-needed resources into their families and communities, or that challenge power structures that have oppressed and exploited the poor of both genders. However, resistance occurs when women compete with men for power in the public sphere, or when they question the power, rights, and privileges of men within the family.

The process of women empowerment must challenge patriarchal relations and thus inevitably leads to change in men's traditional control over women, particularly over the women of their households. Men in communities where such changes have already occurred no longer have control over women's bodies, sexuality, or mobility; they cannot abdicate responsibility for housework and child care, nor physically abuse or violate women with impunity; they cannot abandon or divorce their wives without providing maintenance, or commit bigamy or polygamy, or make unilateral decisions that affect the whole family. Women empowerment also liberates and empowers men, both in material and in psychological terms.

Empowerment helps women to access to the new world of knowledge and can be begin to make new, information choices in both their personnel and public lives. However, such radical changes are not sustainable if limited to a few individual women, because traditional power structures will seek to isolate and ostracise them. Society is forced to change only when large numbers of women are mobilized to press for change. The empowerment process must organize women into collectives, breaking out from individual isolation and creating, a united forum through which women can challenge their subordination. With the support of the collective and the activist agent, women can re-examine their lives critically, recognize the structures and sources of power and sub-ordination, discover their strengths, and initiate action.

The process of empowerment is thus a spiral, changing consciousness, identifying areas to target for change, planning strategies, acting for change, and analyzing action and outcomes, which leads in turn to higher levels of consciousness and more finely honed and better executed strategies. The empowerment spiral affects everyone involved; the individual, the activist agent, the collective, and the community. Thus, empowerment cannot be a top-down or one-way process. Armed with a new consciousness and growing collective strength, women begin to assert their right to control resources including their own bodies and to participate equally in decisions within the family, community, and village. Present day notions of power have evolved in hierarchal, male-dominated societies and are based on divisive, destructive, and oppressive values. The point is not for women to take power and use it in the same exploitative and corrupt way.

Rather, women empowerment processes must evolve a new understanding of power, and experiment with ways of democratizing and sharing power-building new mechanisms for collective responsibility, decision-making, and accountability. Similarly, once women have gained control over resources, they should not use them in the same short-sighted and ecologically destructive manner as male-dominated capitalist societies. There are three major identifiable approaches to women empowerment:

> "Becoming Powerful" the liberal meaning of the term "empowerment" is being used today in all spheres of life as a process to strengthen the elements of society. It is both a process and the result of the process. It is transformation of the structures or institutions that reinforces and perpetuates gender discrimination. It is a process that enables women to gain access to and control of material as well as information resources. Gender disparity manifests itself in various forms, the most obvious being the trend of declining female ratio in population. The 'empowerment' approach was first clearly articulated in 1985 by Development Alternatives with Women for a New Era (DAWN). This term received prominence in early nineties in Western Countries. In India the Central Government in its welfare programmes shifted the concept of development to empowerment only in the Ninth Plan (1997-2002) and observed the year 2001 as "Women Empowerment Year".

The conceptual model for empowerment conceived by M.C. Pillai (2000) encompasses five distinct stages. According to him, awareness building is the fundamental step towards their empowerment. This is followed by education and training in technology and management. While general education accelerate the problems of awareness building, technical education improves skill and dexterity which in-turn promote capacity building process. When this is supplied by adequate funding, the problem concerned is put to stabilization path. This ultimately leads to expansion and diversification.

Empowerment of women implies several things like recognizing their contribution and knowledge, helping to fight against their own fears and feelings of inadequacy and inferiority, enhancing their self respect and dignity, controlling their own bodies, becoming economically independent and self-reliant, controlling resources like land and property, reducing their burden of work, creating and strengthening group and organizations and finally promoting qualities of nurturing, caring and gentleness not just in women but also to men (Kamala Bhasin, 1992).

Thus, empowerment is meant to become self-dependent through recognizing their knowledge which will give them self-confidence, dignity and commanding power. The other aspect in this regard is to become aware of one's own power to fight against the injustice and exploitation towards them. This is possible through the collective efforts of women. This collective action will transform poor women from being weak to being strong which makes them more egalitarian, more just, most free, more honest, more democratic, etc. Single village-level groups of women is the base for such collectivism, but for widespread fundamental change, women's group would be linked together, which is the main facet of women empowerment.

Therefore, empowerment is considered as the initial phase of women's liberation, freedom and equality. It is a first step in a long journey towards the formulation and the realization of human rights and the responsibility that transcend gender role stereo-type and the objectification of women and the men (Everette, 1993). Empowerment is the expansion of assets and capabilities of poor people to participate in negotiate with, influence, control, and hold accountable institution that affect their lives (Narayan, 2002).

Literally, empowerment denotes 'to invest with power'. But, women's empowerment is much broader in connotation. It is not limited to a specific area which has stretched the biological differences to inequalities in the culture and strengthened the prejudices by the erroneous socialization process. In physical power men might be superior to women but this has been wrongly utilized to consider women as inferior in every respect; physical as well as psychological.

The concept of empowerment of women aims at rectifying such misperceptions and generates an environment where women will have the psychological potency to overcome the discriminations. Simultaneously, it is directed to transform the prejudiced norms guiding the society. The psychological domain is strengthened by physical capabilities and empowerment includes social, economic, legal and political dimensions. It is a process of transforming one's life situation by gaining control over the environment external as well as internal. Its emphasizes is on improvement of women's decision-making capabilities, defence against discrimination, independent income, non-discriminatory legal and political rights, a capacity to assert against patriarchal norms justifying gender differences at the individual as well as social levels.

Empowerment is about people—both women and men—taking control over their lives: becoming consciousness of their own situation and position, setting their own agendas, creating space for themselves, gaining skills, building self-confidence, solving problems, and developing self-reliance. It is not only a social and political process, but also an individual one as well and it is not only a process but an outcome too.

The nature of empowerment renders it difficult to define. On the one hand, it is often referred as a goal for many development programmes projects. On the other hand, it can also be conceived as a process that people undergo, which eventually leads to changes. Nelly Stromquist, for instance, defines empowerment as "a process to change the distribution of power both in interpersonal relations and in institutions throughout society". While Lucy Lazo describes it as, "process of acquiring, providing, bestowing the resources and the means or enabling the access to a control over such means of resources".

MEASURES OF EMPOWERMENT

Empowerment is a planned and its nature and quality of relationship over time can be assessed. Changes in power relations were a definite part of the empowerment process. There was a tendency to progress from dependency through independence towards increased interdependence. It is not difficult to measure empowerment; but the difficulty lies in achieving it.

The Gender Empowerment Measure (GEM) used variables constructed explicitly to measure the relative empowerment of women and men in political and economic spheres of activities namely, participation, decision-making and power over resources. Any meaningful attempt to measure empowerment would have to go beyond measuring the transfer of resources (physical, financial, human) to the least powerful. Generally, empowerment is considered as development skills to make a person more confident, self-reliant and to develop ability to take self-decisions.

Empowerment is a process of strengthening or enhancing the authority or autonomy by giving information, delegation of responsibility and offering share in decision-making so that the performance in different sectors of the improves. Empowerment makes an individual an able organizer and a good employee, that is, worker in a work setting. Empowerment refers broadly in the expansion of freedom of choice and action to shape one's life. It implies control over resources and decisions. For women, their being voiceless and powerless in relation to the State and markets severely curtail that freedom. There are important gender inequalities, including within the household, since powerlessness is embedded in a culture of unequal institutional relations.

Empowerment refers to enabling people to take charge of their lives. For women, empowerment emphasizes the importance of increasing their power and taking control over decisions and issues that shape their lives.

Women empowerment addresses power and relationships in society interviewed with gender, class, race, ethnicity, age, culture and history. Power is identified with equity and equality for women and men in access to resources, participation in decision-making and control over distribution of resources and benefits. Gender equality is addressed at these different levels with the aim of increasing equality between men and women, and achieving women empowerment. Access to resources refers to both the means and the right to obtain services, products or commodities. Gender gaps in access to resources and services are a major obstacle to women's development. The process of empowerment includes mobilizing women to eliminate these gaps. A cornerstone of gender equality is women's equal participation in decision-making.

To empower women literally speaking is to give power to women. 'Power' here does not mean a mode of domination over others, but a sense of internal strength and confidence to face life, the right to determine one's choices in life, the ability to influence the social processes that affect one's life, an influence in the direction of social change, a share in decision-making and capacity building to contribute towards national development. Empowerment is the expansion of assets and capabilities of women to participate in, negotiate with, influence, control and hold accountable institutions that affect their lives.

Since poverty is multi-dimensional women need a range of assets and capabilities at the individual levels such as health, education and housing and at the collective level such as the ability to organize and mobilize to take collective action to solve their problems. Empowering women requires the removal of formal and informal institutional barriers that prevent them from taking action to improve their well-being individually or collectively—and limit their choices. The key formal institutions include the laws, rules and regulations upheld by States, markets, civil society and international agencies; informal institutions include norms of social solidarity, sharing, social exclusion and corruption among others.

In order to measure and monitor empowerment, it is important to have a clear definition of the concept and to specify a framework that both links empowerment to improved development outcomes and identifies determinants of empowerment itself.

Empowerment refers broadly to the expansion of freedom of choice and action to shape one's life. It implies control over resources and decisions. For poor people, that freedom is severely curtailed by their powerlessness in relation to a range of institutions, both formal and informal. Since, powerlessness is embedded in a culture of unequal institutional relations an institutional definition of empowerment has been adopted.

- Women and men's sense of internal strength and confidence to face life.
- The right to make choices.
- The power to control their lives within and outside the home.
- The ability to influence the direction of social and economic changes towards the creation of a more just social and economic orders nationally and internationally.

Stromquist (1995), in her article on educational empowerment for women, interprets empowerment as a "socio-political concept that goes beyond formal political participation and consciousness rising. She argues that a full definition of empowerment must include cognitive, psychological, political and economic components". She explains that:

- The cognitive component refers to women having an understanding of the conditions and causes of their subordination at micro and macro-levels. It involves making choices that may go against cultural expectations and norms.
- The economic component requires that women have access to and control over productive resources, thus ensuring some degree of financial autonomy.. However, she notes that changes in the economic balance of power do not necessarily alter traditional gender roles or norms.
- The political entails that women have the capability to analyze, organize and mobilize for social change.
- The psychological component includes the belief that women can act at personal and social levels to improve their individual realities and the society in which they live.

Empowerment denoted a process of acquiring, providing, bestowing the resources and the means or enabling the access to and control over such means and resources. This implies that the individual has a potential to acquire power upon her own initiative or that another party could make it possible for her to have power. This point is vital because it identifies the potential agents of empowerment: it is the person who is to be empowered or it could be another person or agent. Empowerment could be a self-propelled and self-propelling process. If by some gift of God, it dawns on a woman that her life could become better if she tried to act upon such thoughts, link up with the source of resources, then she is facilitating her own empowerment.

Empowerment enables the person to gain insight and have awareness of what is undesirable and unfavourable about her current situation, perceive a better situation, the possibilities of attaining it and realising what is within her reach and what she could do to get to a better situation. This characterisation of empowerment implies that the process could involve a change of perceptions about the self, the environment, and the relationship of the self and the environment. It is a process that involves the creation of images, the generation of a "push" to act or what psychologists call motivation. Change of perceptions implies a change of attitude and a change in one's outlook in life.

Empowerment enables women to generate choices and as an outcome of having such choices, she acquires leverage and bargaining power. Empowered, a woman could take steps to find and or create options or find and link to the means to find the options. It makes a person able to choose and able to demand. It makes the person able to choose her goals, generate opportunities to reach the goals and determine the overall direction of her life. This makes the notion of empowerment a fascinating and powerful one.

In the Third World, some women have on possibility to choose their own life goals and this indicates a state of powerfulness. We are aware for instance of societies and tribes where women are committed to marriage by their parents even before they are born or ready for it. By the norm of their society, this mode of behaviour is acceptable; yet it may women has no choice and is therefore powerless under the situation. Here is to obey and not to protest.

Empowerment enables a woman to gain relative strength as a result of having choices and bargaining power. The consequences could be reduction of invisibility as she is able to demand attention from those concerned, especially decision and policy-makers, to generate the appropriate positive responses, reduction of vulnerability, reduction or elimination of exploitability, availability and of social services and resources. Ultimately, empowerment should lead to the improvement of women's socio-economic status.

Empowerment is the acquisition or the bestowing of power. The variables of power are the variables of empowerment as well. Power is a complex quality that gives the person the authority and the strength to exercise control and influence. Power arises from possessing a complex combination of personal and physical resources that is being bestowed or being acquired in the process of empowerment.

Power implies a relationship. There is one individual or party who possesses a physical, economic, social and or psychological resources and or quality which becomes the basis for the exercise of control and influence over another. Conversely, in the power relationship, there is an individual or party who is the "weaker" whom the other party controls. In layman's parlance, power means having the capacity and the means to direct one's life towards desired social, political and economic goals and or status. It is the ability to influence events and control outcomes in the environment. The crux of power lies in the possession of and/or access to and control over means and resources.

Dimensions of Empowerment

Jo Rowland mentions three dimensions of empowerment. They are:

Personal—developing a sense of self and individual confidence and capacity for undoing the effects of internalize oppression.

Relational—developing the ability to negotiate and influence the nature of a relationship and decisions made within it.

Collective—where individuals work together to achieve a more extensive impact than each could have had alone, collective action is based on co-operation rather than competition.

Santi Rozario (1997) traces the history of the empowerment concept, which she argues has been overused. She divides empowerment into two primary models:

- One model is consistent with Solomon's (1976) approach, which is based on empowering the individual, not on encouraging collective social action by the oppressed.
- The other model is consistent with Paolo Freire's approach, which emphasized conscientization and radical social action.

PROCESS OF WOMEN EMPOWERMENT

The process of empowerment deals with how to empower women and what they need to become empowered. First they must be provided with and should have certain essential needs. These basic needs could be provided through welfare services. Equal access to resources like educational opportunities, credit and property is the next step in the process of empowerment. Creating awareness among women about the existing gender discrimination, gender inequality is most important in empowering them. Then, they must recognize that their problems stem from inherent structural and institutional discrimination.

Equal participation of women in the decision-makings leads to empowerment. It could be achieved through mobilization and organization of women at all levels.

Increasing consciousness and awareness building is the important component of the process of empowerment. First, women must recognize the ideology that legitimizes domination and then understand how it perpetuates their oppression.

They try to change the values and attitudes, which are anti-women that most women have internalized since their childhood. So, self-consciousness and awareness must arise in each individual woman to empower themselves. But, this self-consciousness and awareness does not come spontaneously, so is empowerment. Changing other women consciousness must externally induce it. Altering self-image and beliefs about rights and capabilities could create consciousness among other women. Awareness of gender discrimination challenging the sense of inferiority, recognizing the value of their labour and their contribution to the society and conscientisation will empower women.

Empowerment is an active, multi-dimensional process which should enable women to realize their full identity and powers in all spheres of life. It would consist of greater access the knowledge and resources, greater autonomy in decision-making, greater ability to plan their lives, have greater control over the circumstances that influence their lives and free them from shackles imposed on them by custom, belief and practice. Generally, development with justice is expected to generate the forces that leads to empowerment of various sections of population in a country and to raise their status.

But, power is not a commodity to be transacted. Power can not be given away as alms. Power has to be acquired and once acquired, it needs to be exercised, sustained and preserved. Women have to empower themselves. Unless they themselves become conscious of their oppression, show initiative and seize the opportunities, it would not be possible to change their status.

The empowerment mechanism is easily enumerated:

- Higher literacy and education.
- Better health care for herself and her children.
- Higher age at marriage.
- Greater work participation in modernized sector.

- Necessary financial and service support.
- Advancement into higher position of power.
- Better consciousness of their rights.
- Self-reliance, self-respect and dignity among women.

To World Bank, empowerment is the process of increasing the capacity of individuals or groups to make choices and to transform those choices into desired actions and outcomes. Central to this process was actions which both build individual and collective assets and improve the efficiency and fairness of the organizational and institutional context which govern the use of these assets.

Empowerment as a process of a community or a group there of gaining autonomy and control over one's life. As a result of the empowerment, the empowered should become agents of their own development, exercising choices, selecting their own agenda and changing their status in the society. In the context of gender and development, empowerment should be viewed more as a process than as an end product. It is a dynamic process changing according to circumstances. It applies to the individual as well as the collective. At the individual-level, empowerment involves building up the self-image and self-confidence as well as the critical faculties to think, decide and act. On a collective plan, empowerment means enabling women collectively to take control of their own lives, to set their own agenda, to organize each other and make demands on the state and the society for change.

Conscientization of Women

The process of empowerment begins in the mind, from woman's consciousness, from her very beliefs about herself and her rights, capabilities and potential; from herself image and awareness of how gender as well as other socio-economic and political forces are acting on her; from braking free of the sense of inferiority which has been imprinted since earliest childhood, from recognizing her strength, above all, from believing in her innate right to dignity and justice and realizing that it is she, along with her sisters who must assert that right for no one who holds power will give it away.

Self-actualization

For long women has been living for others sacrificing their ideals and aspiration for the sake of children, family, husband and community. This very often pushed them towards dependency. Women empowerment enables the women to realize their ideals and aspirations. Women are enabled to learn skills and to work to realize their potential.

Social Mobilization of Women

Social mobilization is a process which is induced at the attitudinal and behavior levels in social groups within a society. Individual woman is powerless in many situations hence building groups is the most preferred one for gender solidarity. This solidarity can be utilized for collective action. The most preferred mobilization form nowadays is formation of Self-Help Groups. Self-Help Groups are based on three objectives. They are:

1. Self-Development
2. Social Development
3. Social Action

Social Action

To establish gender equality and justice women have exercise women involving in social action to promote gender parity.

Empowerment as an individual and collective process is based on the following five principles:

- Self-reliance
- Self-awareness
- Collective mobilization and organization
- Capacity building
- External exposure and interaction

Empowerment is a long process. It has to pass through different stages. In the first stage, women should be trained to look into the situation from a different perspective and recognize the power relations that perpetuate their oppression. At this stage, the women share their feelings and experiences with each other and build a common vision and mission. In the second stage, the women tried to change the situation by bringing about a change in the gender and social relations. In the third stage, the process of empowerment makes them more nature to realize the importance of collective action.

As empowerment seeks to alter the gender and power relations, there could be a certain social or gender conflicts. The process of empowerment could also face certain obstacles emanating from the patriarchal system, traditional beliefs and political system. The results of empowerment, however, will not be confined to women. The other member of the families will also benefit from the empowerment process.

While empowerment as a construct has a set of core ideas, it may be defined at different levels: individual, organization, and community; and operationalized in different contexts (Rowlands, 1998). Several working definitions of empowerment are available. However, given the nature of our work, which can be described as directed social change and given the power inequities in societies that are posited as the major impediments to achieving meaningful change, it is important that the working definitions be linked directly to the building and exercise of social power (Speer and Hughey, 1995).

Empowerment is the mechanism by which individuals, organizations and communities gain control and mastery over social and economic conditions (Rappaport, 1984); over democratic participation in their community (Zimmerman and Rappaport, 1988); and over their stories.

As a process, empowerment may have different outcomes. For some it could lead to a perception of control over their lives while for others it may mean actual control (Rappaport, 1987; Young, 1994); it could be an internalized attitude or an externally observable behaviour; it could be an individual achievement; Zimmerman and Rappaport, 1988), a community experience (Chavis and Wandersman, 1990) or a professional intervention using strategies that are informed by local realities. The process itself defies easy definition and may be recognized more easily by its absence: "powerlessness, real or imagined; learned helplessness; and alienation" (Rappaport, 1984).

Usually, a starting point in the process of empowerment is a realization on the part of an individual, group or community of its inequitable position, its powerlessness in the system or the relative neglect of its needs by the larger society.

Objectives of Empowerment

- To find out the present status of women in the society.
- To compare the position/power of women in the past and present society.
- To find out the problem of gender discrimination faced by them.
- To know about the hindrances that prevented their opportunities for better development.
- To know about their ways of approach in their problematic situations and how they tackled it.
- To find out the origin and history of self-help group.
- To evaluate their socio-economic status after they joined in self-help groups.
- To know about their psychological feelings while they are appreciated and given chances to participate in decision-making by their family members.
- To know whether the self-help group has created awareness about gender-based discrimination among its members.
- To know whether the self-help group has motivated its members to take affirmative actions against perceived exploitation by others.
- To know whether self-help group members are economically empowered.
- To measure the self-help group members participation in public spheres.

The aims of empowerment may be different for different groups, "It may merely aim at improving women's income, health or eradication of social evils like dowry, child marriages, etc. or it may deal with questioning gender relations and power equations. It is those who are involving in empowering women have to decide which is the most urgent". (Srilatha Batliwala, 1995).

The empowerment process is one where women find time and space of their own and begin to re-examine their life critically and collectively. Double burden and drudgery of work should be reduced to and let them have their time to think about themselves and observe what is happening around them.

Empowerment process starts from one woman either individually or collectively and then reaches other women so it is rather a horizontal approach than top down approach. Besides, women alone cannot undertake the process of empowerment; men must be involved in the process. Otherwise it would become like clap with one hand. "Along with women, men must undergo a process of reflection and transformation which makes it possible for them to recognizes the ways in their power is a double edged sword" (Kate Young, 1993).

"If the aim of the empowerment is transforming the society, then it should be undertaken as a political movement by challenging the existing power structure and gender relations that oppressed and subordinate the women. It should generate new structure of power which involves equity, sharing, giving, creating and developing the potentiality of every human being, as the present structure of power is hierarchical, exploitative destructive and aggressive. It should not lead to taking over the men's power and perpetuate the same exploitative and hierarchical structure. It should create a world of equality and make best use of potentially of all human beings in constructing the more human world". (Kate Young, 1993).

According to J.K. Pillai, "it is necessary to restructure all aspects of society in order to empower women. Power to empower cannot be given as alms but it has to be acquired. Once acquired it needs to be exercised, sustained and reserved". (J.K. Pillai, 1989). Outside intervention may do all efforts by providing welfare, development scheme, and legal protection and there by reduce the hurdles and create an atmosphere conducive to transformation, but it is the women who have to take steps and empower themselves. Unless they themselves realize that they are oppressed, show initiates and seize opportunities it would not be possible to empower them.

It is argued that empowerment as the product of development thinking has become more capitalistic-oriented concentrated on increasing income, self-employment with profit motive, marketing the products, etc. So, "emerging as a concept of mainstream development theory and practice women's empowerment means building entrepreneurial self-reliance through capitalism and market forces. It emphasized individualistic values and expects women to empower by pulling themselves up. It does not talk about co-operation and changing the existing social structure". (Kate Young, 1993).

The empowerment aspect of development thinking does not

make men, who have financial and political power obligatory to change themselves. It continued them to hold power, which makes women powerless. So, our efforts should be to change both men and women if our aim is to establish an egalitarian society. Once we know that is empowerment and as a process what it involves, then the question is how to achieve it and to decide what are the strategies and approaches adopted and to be adopted in the process of empowerment. The process of empowerment of women must start from the family and then extend to outside the family. Equal treatment by family member, visibility to household work, share of household work, consulting in family matters, encouragement to participate in social activities, choices and decision-making power regarding education, marriage, work, etc. would create an environment for women to empower themselves.

Women must be aware of their subordination caused by gender, caste, class and structure and organize themselves to fight the sources of subordination then they can empower themselves. So, emphasis was made and should be made in future also for creating awareness and organizing women in changing women's self-image. "Unless women are free from their existing perception of themselves as weak, inferior and limited beings, no amount of external intervention will enable them to channelise the existing power equation in the society". (Srilatha Batliwala, 1995).

Another important reason for the disempowerment of women is absence of women in historical records, which has made their contribution and role invisible. Historical records were documented and studied research has done in various disciplines without recognizing women. Identifying their contribution, developing role models, exposing the real facts on women through surveys, studies, research, evaluations, developing new research methodology and reading material would help in empowering women. Besides lobbies and advocacies have to be made to draw attention of national and international agencies for intervening in the process of empowerment of women.

The important objectives of empowerment are the following:

- To develop sense of internal strength and self-confidence to face life,
- To improve the performances by delegating responsibility,

- To give authority or autonomy to choose and to make self-decisions,
- To enhance the participation in decision-making at all levels,
- To influence in the direction of social change, and
- To contribute towards national development.

Year Plan and Empowerment

Women in India are still a neglected lot, despite the assurance given in the constitution and commitment towards women empowerment. They are poorest of the poor receiving little education, low medical attention, lower value for their work, take the remainder of the food basket of the household; but still they are over burdened with all the domestic drudgery ranging from collecting collective firewood, drinking water and cooking in an adverse house environment. They are still subjected to frequent pregnancies resulting in pregnancy wastage and increasing risk of maternal mortality. With all these adverse circumstances at the domestic front, their contribution to the production in the firm as well as on the farm is in no way inferior to the men folk.

In India, it was assumed that trickledown effect of rapid economic growth would improve the quality of life of the downtrodden and weaker sections of the population. It was realized that unless exclusive women development programmes are initiated, women's development would not be possible. In India, the era of development of Indian women was started with the appointment of a committee on the status of women in 1971 to examine the rights and status of women in the context of changing social and economic conditions in the country. Influenced by the declaration of the year 1975 as the International Women's Year and the decade of 1975-85 as the International Women's Decade, Government of India designed the Fifth Five Year Plan (1974-79) for implementing certain policies and programmes to achieve advancement of women and to eliminate discrimination.

The Sixth Plan (1980-85) was formulated against the background of the report of the committee on the status of women in India, "Towards Equality". It was pointed out that the low status of women in large segments of Indian society cannot be raised without opening up opportunities of independent employment and income for them, as such Development of Women and Children in

Rural Areas (DWCRA) was started a pilot project in 50 Districts in 1982-83 in the country, Sixth Plan strategy for women's development was three-fold: education, employment and health.

In the Seventh Plan (1985-90) the identification and promotion of beneficiary-oriented programmes for women in different developmental sectors have been implemented in order to bring them into the mainstream of national development. Further, the plan proposed to increase the participation of women in Integrated Rural Development Programme, National Rural Employment Programme and Rural Landless Employees Guarantee Programme.

The Eighth Plan (1992-97) makes a paradigm shift from 'women's development' to 'women empowerment'. This has come a long way by way of moving from growth to growth with equity, from bureaucratic delivery of services to people's participation, from economic development to human development and from asset and services endowment to empowerment.

The Ninth Plan (1997-2002) is attempting another experiment of shifting the focus from household-based to community-based programmes. Nothing the success of DWCRA in A.P. in organizing women for income generating activities and promoting the habit of saving, the World Bank is coming forward to implement poverty alleviation programmes through women's organization at the grassroots level.

The advancement, development and empowerment of women are the central issue in the context of social development. In India, the constitution forbids the State from practicing any form of gender-based discrimination and holds it responsible for achieving gender equality in all fields. It has also to undertake special measures wherever necessary to eliminate all forms of discrimination or disparity.

Women all over the world today are breaking barriers and providing that they are inferior to none. In India, whether it is Politics or Administration or Justice or Technology or Diplomacy or Management or Teaching, women have proved their competence and worth, time and again. One of the challenges of sustainable development today, is to convert these rare achievements to an universal common pattern.

Indian women play an extremely critical role in sustaining survival systems. Their empowerment has always helped the advancement of the family and the community. At the present juncture, when the Indian economy and society are undergoing fast changes, it is imperative to bring these activities of women to the centre stage in planning of people-oriented public development programme.

While affirmative actions will have to be continued if this is to be achieved, a grim reminder of the low status of women is the declining sex ratio in the country. The sex ratio that was 972 females per thousand males in 1901 has declined to 927 in 1991. The decline has been more or less steady over the decades, except for a marginal rise between 1941 and 1951 and a small rise, more recently, between 1971 and 1981.

Other more recent indicators of human development and gender empowerment such as participation in economic and political structures are similarity adverse for women. Making women equal partners in the national development processes and equipping them to make informed choices in order to actualize their self-worth through empowerment are goals to which the Government is committed. There is a long way to go, but the endeavour is ceaseless.

The major strategy for the Ninth Plan will be to bring a holistic approach to women's development. This underscores harmonization of various efforts in different fronts—social, economic, legal, political and cultural. This calls for consolidation of various programmes and efforts in different sectors of the Government and their integration in a logical fashion to converge various services and facilities required by women. A sub-Plan approach to package all relevant resources and benefits for women's development will be laid down to ensure their systematic focus on women.

The over arching strategy component for women's development in the Nineth Plan will comprise mobilization and convergence orchestrated by women's groups and supported by Panchayati Raj institutions. The organization of women will by itself empower them and provide them a forum for articulating their needs and contributing their perspectives to development. This will also give them experience in participatory decision-making, thereby building up a cadre of grass-root leaders, capable of effective participation in institutions of local Government.

The credit delivery system for the rural and urban women will also be strengthened by increasing the corpus and reach of the

Rashtriya Mahila Kosh (RMK) and the Women Development Corporations (WDCs).

Mahila Samriddhi Yojana will be continued and more structure will be built on it during the Ninth Plan. This scheme will be linked with Indira Mahila Yojana (IMY) and RMK. Formation of MSY, Self-Help Group (SHG) and MSY Awareness Generation Clubs will be encouraged with the help of IMKs, IMBSs and NGOs.

Credit at the door step of the rural women will be ensured by providing adequate funds to the Rashtriya Mahila Kosh, Indira Mahila Block Societies will be used as extended arms of the RMK for this purpose and IMBSs will also become conduits for all other credit schemes for rural women. With the involvement of IMBS in the credit activities, the reach of RMK and other schemes with similar aims will increase considerably. RMK should handle over Rs.1000 crores during the Ninth Plan for reaching credit to large number of women's groups.

The Women's Development Corporation can also on their own take up a variety of other activities which seek to improve the earning capacity of women, make credit available and provide link up with marketing networks. For this purpose WDC's should provide training in collaboration with various institutes or follow the syllabus recognized by such institutes so that trainees are eligible for appearing in professional tests. WDC's should try to create linkages with other agencies so that there is regular demand for the products of training-*cum*-production centers. They may also play an important role in making credit available to women by establishing linkages with banks as well as by providing margin money to such women.

Economic Empowerment of Women

The economic status of women guides their social status. The economic status itself derives substantially from their empowerment. It is well recognized that women do not form a homogeneous group and the perceptions of women belonging to different class and culture segments vary distinctly. While women in households forming the lowest deciles of the income segments may perceive their status improvement in getting more time for leisure, the women in a different class or culture segment relate their improved status to an opportunity to work and earn.

Another index of economic status is asset ownership. Socio-cultural traditions world over favour male ownership of assets, particularly immovable property and land, except in matriarchal societies. The laws relating to inheritance vary between different religious sections. Progressive legislations have brought some access to property for women by providing equal share for sons and daughters as in the case of the Hindu Succession Act. Yet women's access to assets is not universal, and the implementation of the law has not captured the spirit of the legislation. The declining sex ratio in some parts of the country is even noticed as a reaction to the threats of claims to the family property by the daughters.

Another factor in economic empowerment is the participation of women in decision-making with regard to raising, application and distribution of resources, that is, incomes, investments and expenditure at all levels starting from the household to the state and national levels. Women are yet in search of their economic empowerment.

At the house-hold level women provide care and largely engage themselves in processing and distributing food at the household-level. In certain cases they are main bread-winners and according to the NSSO 1993, 34% of the households are women headed. Neither in cases where they are bread-winners nor where they are the provider of food to the family are they fully associated with decision-making on the disposal of family resources including assets and incomes. This is a factor closely related to the social status of women starting from the household to the highest decision-making bodies at the national level.

The economic empowerment of women hinges largely on her economic status which is related to her income earning ability. The universal reality is that work done for the household is not counted as adding an income to the household and therefore not considered as economic contribution to the nation. Most work for the care and nature of the family is done by women like cooking, washing, cleaning, fetching water, fuel and fodder, nursing the sick and the young, which do not get counted as paid work bringing income to the family and the nation. Consequently, the unpaid works of the women do not give her an economic status in the family or society.

At the same time, the level of economic participation of women is taken as an indicator of women's development in a society and their development score is viewed as low, where the work participation rate for women is low.

For poverty alleviation and improving the incomes of household in all economic strata and for optimum use of human resources, employment of women has become a critical issue. The magnitude of the problem is disguised due to under and unemployment prevailing in the economy for men and women. The major thrust of economic growth is to provide full employment to all. Special efforts and affirmative action is necessary for reducing unemployment for women and increasing their access to greater employment and higher incomes. The Ninth Five Year Plan that coincides with economic policy transitions needs to pay special attention to the distinctive characteristics of women's employment but to give them economic status and employment with equal remunerations.

An overall representation of women in the labour force still remains low for various reasons such as change in the definition of 'workers' since 1981 census. Low percentage of workers may also reflect a higher capacity of the working population to support a large number of the dependents and may be due to growing magnitude of unemployment in general. In other words, the low level of female work participation is due more to the invisibility of women's economic activity rather than their lack of involvement.

Women's work is invisible because women are confined to unpaid work in the family enterprises. Much of women's economic activity is unrecognized even by women themselves and is unreported by heads of households and thus unrecorded in the census. Further, women's access to many important areas in industry is constrained by their low levels of literacy, education and technical skills. Those women who do work lend to be employed as casual workers in non-formal activities where they are unprotected by legislation or trade unions and often work under conditions that endanger their health and safety.

Ninty six percent of women workers are engaged in the informal sector—often working from their homes, unprotected by labour laws and legislations. Much of their work remains unrecognized and grossly under-remunerated. This has an adverse impact on their status in society, and the opportunities they have in public life. While it is true that women the world-over do not have the same opportunities as men do, extreme poverty and the low levels of education bring out the harshest aspects of their discrimination. The poor status of women in India is most tellingly reflected in the declining number of females per thousand of males from 972 in 1901 to 923 in 2001.

The adverse sex ratio is also a reflection of other forms of disparity that exists between men and women in the Indian society. The female literacy and enrolment rates are considerably inferior to those of men. The female literacy rate was 53.6% in 1991 compared with 64.8% for men. Even among women there is considerably difference in the rural and urban areas. The literacy rate is 30.62% in rural areas, less than half the rate of 64.05% in urban areas.

Despite these handicaps, if women, who collect fuel and fodder or work in dairy, poultry or kitchen gardening are added to those in the conventionally defined labour force, women participation rates goes up to 51%, which is only 13% below the rate for men. In addition, women take upon themselves the basic duties of house-keeping. The distribution of female main workers by industrial categories shows that 80% of women engaged in agricultural and allied activities, 3.53% in household industry, 3.9% in manufacturing and processing outside the household industry while 2.26% were in trade and commerce.

While liberalization, stabilization and structural adjustment employment generation in the public sector has at best been marginal in recent years. The informal sector will, therefore, continue to be crucial as far as employment opportunities for women are concerned.

The female work participation rate declines sharply from illiterate to literate groups up to the middle level and rises again for secondary and high educational levels. This reflects the prevailing socio-cultural attitudes to employment in our country where higher education actually has a negative impact on work participation rates of women at least up to middle school level. Only education above the middle school level has an equalizing effect on male and female work participation rates.

It is noteworthy that a significant portion of the contribution of women in the economy remains invisible. Despite, long hours of work and significant contribution to the family income women are not perceived as workers either by themselves or the data collecting agencies and the Government. The multi-dimensional activities of women remain un-recognized and un-reported. A large number of women are employed as casual labourers in construction industry where they are dependent on the contractors for employment who usually exploit them through loan bondage.

The plight of the huge female labour force engaged in the plantation sector is similar. In the north-eastern States and Kerala, women comprise 50-90% of the workers in tea plantation. In other States also women are largely engaged in production of cash crops such as potato, tobacco, apples and other fruits, etc. However, women generally have to encounter various obstacles in their pursuit of employment due to family responsibilities, limited mobility and social restrictions. Lack of access to means of production, ownership of land, other productive assets, technological skills, credit and marketing facilities, etc. makes their task even more onerous.

In keeping with this overall approach to economic development through decentralization, the strategic thrust of the Department of Women and Child Development during the recent years has been towards building the capacity of the community. Empowerment of women through facilitating formation of Self-Help Groups at village level and providing such groups the resources to enable them to organize income-generating activities is considered essential to building the capacity of the community. This is the genesis of the schemes that seek to bring out the convergence of the country's development efforts of the grass-roots level through schemes such as Indira Mahila Yojana (IMY). For ensuring cost effective and efficient utilization of resources in the social sector, convergence of inter-sectoral services has been identified as the thrust area of our economic planning.

Another inadequacy and organizing the SHGs at the grass-root levels to benefit through convergence of various states sponsored schemes has been the inadequacy of infrastructure facilities at the village level. Probably, the only common facilities available all over the country are the Anganwadis under the ICDS projects located at the village level, and the majority of even these do not have a building of their own. If the efforts to converge the various social sector schemes at the village levels were to succeed, at the very least a common location in the form of a building and other associated infrastructure would have to be provided. Development of infrastructure facilities in a broader sense would of course include provision of banking facilities, educational opportunities and channels of acquisition of raw materials for production and marketing of products made by these SHGs.

The skill development and employment promotion schemes implemented by the different agencies had very limited coverage compared to the galloping numbers of job-seekers emerging in the labour market. The linkages of these schemes with markets for services and products were weak, resulting in serious problems of marketing the products or getting absorbed in jobs. Thirdly, the design of the skill development programmes seems to be deficient in some ways as they do not equip the trainee to orient her product at quality levels desired by the market. Fourth, there are mismatches between employment opportunities and skills available which have not been scientifically studied to integrate various programmes in a holistic manner to cope with changing technological and cultural developments in the society. Fifth, linkages with credit continued as a weak link, despite a plethora of these programmes, and women's access to credit from the Banking sector remained insignificant. Sixth, entrepreneurial development among women remained at a low level and the opportunities were inadequate.

The Women Development Corporations established in the States, which have the responsibility of promoting women's employment by accessing the required resources, have themselves been languishing without appropriate manpower and adequate resources. Consequently, their role has been limited in catalyzing women's employment.

During the past half-a-century, India has witnessed a positive transformation in women empowerment and economic development while retaining a great diversity in its political and social system. Although, India still has to go a long way in attaining gender equality and gender justice, no one can deny that its efforts towards redressing gender inequality are more pronounced than in many other countries.

In recent time, the empowerment of women has emerged as an important issue in our society. Though the empowerment of women is not absolutely a new phenomenon in almost all societies throughout the world, but the concept is considered a new for its increasingly discussion and occupation of a place of prominence in public due to its having been shifted and reshaped from women's welfare to their overall development and to now the name of women empowerment. There has been increasingly realization and recognition that empowerment of women is absolutely essential for familial, societal, national and global development and progress.

For this reason, it has been realized and accepted that genuine commitment and efforts have to be made by political thinkers, academicians, administrators, Government and Non-Government organizations to work towards establishing women empowerment issue as national and international matter of discussion. The ultimate goal of empowering women is to provide an increased awareness of their rights and duties, equal participation and status in almost all spheres with men including opportunities and freedom to developed herself and ending violence or atrocities committed against them.

A fair access to resources is essential for empowering women without which the confidence to fight against discrimination cannot be strengthened. There is an organic inter-winning between empowerment of women and feminism, which denounced gender-based inequalities and evolved the ameliorative measures at the operational level in the society to mutate the life situation of women. Empowerment has been its most effective means to achieve its objectives in the mid-nineties of the 20th century.

APPROACHES FOR WOMEN EMPOWERMENT

Empowerment has multi-dimensional approaches. We can identify five important approaches. They are education, economic, development, consciousness raising organizational approaches, increasing political participation can also be one of the approaches. (N.K. Banerjee, 1995).

Education Approach

Illiteracy among women has become an obstacle to the development and empowerment of women and to achieve gender equality. Education has been considered to be the prime means of empowering women. Education creates awareness, helps to acquire knowledge and information, and equips women with ability to analyze and assess their situation and gain courage to change it. It also helps them to challenge oppressive behaviour, to organize they and to educate their children. So, the first approach to empower women is to make them literate and educate them. Literacy and education opens the possibility of unlimited exposure to new information and also new ways of thinking and new perspective on existing information. (Sushma Sahay, 1998).

Education is a step toward the empowerment as it improves the health and nutritional status, enable them to take decisions regarding marriage, number of children, education of children and to acquire economic independence. Empowerment through education will lead to greater participation in economic and political fields and even in Government and community institutions, increasing their choices and opportunities.

Economic Approach

Economic approach starts with recognizing and revaluing women's work. One of the reasons for their subordination is that women's work unpaid and underpaid. Lack of control over material resources, lack of education, skills, training has caused women economic insecurity so there is greater need for access to and control over resources, skill development through training, savings and credit facilities to bring economic empowerment of women. Those who are earning must have control over their income. Organization of women, forming and undertaking group activities, establishing thrift groups, providing financial existence, encouraging self-employment, etc. are the strategies for economic empowerment. Compiling and collecting accurate data on women's work, entry of women into money market, more employment opportunities, equal pay for equal work and various development programmes are aimed at economic empowerment of women.

Development Approach

In this approach efforts have been made to integrate women into the process of development. At the beginning, emphasis was on poverty alleviation providing basic needs. Later, the emphasis has been shifted to remove gender discrimination towards improving self-efficiency. Gender concerns have been incorporated in development planning and activities. The development approach ascribes women's powerlessness to their greater poverty and lower access to health care, education and survival resources. (Sushma Sahay, 1998). Development strategies are focused on providing services and enhancing economic as well as social status.

Consciousness Raising Approach

This approach asserts that women empowerment requires awareness of empowerment. This requires awareness of the complex factors causing women's subordination. This approach organizes women into collective group that tackle the sources of subordination. They must recognize the existing gender gaps or inequalities and realize that they are due to structural and institutional discrimination. They must also understand the existing gender relations and how they affect the status of women, socialization, gender sensitization, gender planning, altering the self-image and beliefs about the rights and responsibilities lead to consciousness raising and thereby to empowerment of women.

Organizational Approach

Empowerment through organization is the most recent and popular approach. The approach raises basic survival needs as the priority development issue and also pushes for major structural changes at the policy level. Srilatha Batliwala says, "it is difficult for one woman to bring lasting change, but if whole group of women begin to demand change, it much more difficult for society to reject them altogether". It is forced to acknowledge, respond to and accommodate them as best as possible. Strategies of organizational approaches focus more on organizing women to recognize and challenge both gender and class-based discrimination in all aspects of lives in both the public and private lives. (Sushma Sahay, 1998). To deal with social problems, getting financial assistance and skills training, to resist patriarchal norms which are anti-women, to get information and knowledge and to participate in decision-making organizational approach is a mean of achieving empowerment.

Political Approach

An environment, which could increase women's political participation, should be created. Politics, which is free from violence, character assassination and unscrupulous struggles for power, should be established. Knowledge, information, exposure to various experiments, training and encouragement from the family should be provided to equip women to participate actively in the politics.

Empowerment is a word widely used, but seldom defined. Long before the word became popular, women were speaking about gaining control over their lives and participating decisions that affect them in the home and community, in Government and international development policies. The word 'empowerment' captures this sense of gaining control, of participating, of decision-making. More recently, the word has entered the vocabulary of development agencies, including international organizations and the United Nations (Karl, 1995).

Integrated Development Approach

This approach ascribes women's powerlessness to their greater poverty and lower access to health care, education, and survival resources. Strategies are focused on providing services and enhancing economic status; some Non-Governmental Organizations (NGOs) also emphasize awareness building. This approach improves women's condition mainly by helping them meet their survival and livelihood needs.

Economic Development Approach

This place women's economic vulnerability at the centre of their powerlessness, and posits that economic empowerment has a positive impact on other aspects of women's existence. Its strategies are built around strengthening women's position as workers and income earners by mobilizing, organizing or unionizing and providing access to support services.

Consciousness—Raising and Organizing Approach

This approach is based on a more complex understanding of gender relations and women's status. Strategies focus more on organizing women to recognize and challenge both gender and class-based discrimination in all aspects of their lives, in both the public and the private spheres. Women are mobilized to struggle for greater access to resources, rather than passively provided with schemes and services. This approach is successful in enabling women to address their position and strategic needs, but may not be as effective in meeting immediate needs.

These are not mutually exclusive categories, but they help to distinguish among the differing interpretations of the causes of women's powerlessness and hence, among the different interventions thought to lead to empowerment.

Empowerment strategies must intervene at the level of women's 'condition' while also transforming their 'position', thus simultaneously addressing both practical and strategic needs.

Whether it is empowerment in general or women empowerment in particular the concept, as understood from the above definitions is related to power and control over resources and self. Achieving equality, decision-making power, gaining confidence, building productive capacities, challenging existing power relations, gaining control over resources are the essential components which an individual or a group has to achieve through the process of empowerment.

Strategies

Empowerment can be activated through five strategies: Education to promote the level of awareness, knowledge, information and skills of a woman is an important part of the strategy. Awareness is a pre-requisite for challenging the forces of oppression *status que*. It results in greater participation of women in decision-making with in and outside the family.

The economic approach to empowerment seeks to alter the economic status of women by attacking the forces which cause gender division of labour, gender gap in wages, lack of control for women over their material resources, etc. The economic approach emphasizes development of women's skills, promotion of their savings and investment and enlarged economic opportunities.

The third approach namely, development approach attributes poverty to their powerlessness and the lack of adequate access to health care, education and services resources.

Yet another approach believes that women empowerment requires awareness of a complex factors causing disempowerment of women. This approach advocates collective organization of women as well as gender sensitization, gender planning and strategy and consciousness raising activities. More recently, an organizational approach has been advocated which believes that organized women can alter the gender and social relations in favour of women both in public and private lives.

Finally, political approaches to empowerment believes that women can be developed on par with men, if politics are purged of violence, electoral malpractices, unscrupulous struggles, etc. and were made value-based. This would, however, require greater participation of women in active politics.

Empowerment could take place at two levels, individual and collective. Individual empowerment is a process of personal empowerment involving self-esteem, dignity, self-respect and self-perception. But, the problems affecting the collectively of women require collective empowerment. Restructuring power relations, changing social values and norms require intervention at the collective level. Collective empowerment aims at transforming collecting consciousness, values and attitudes. The problem of securing better access to education skills and employment, material resources and political power can be tackled only at the collective level. This requires effective organization among women, mutual help and certain amount of sacrifice.

Self-reliance requires acquisition of physical and mental strength through solidarity, sharing and caring for each other. Self-awareness, on the other hand implies knowledge of living conditions and the factors promoting those conditions. Collectivization and organization therefore are called for to change the living conditions through collective effort, pooling and sharing of resources, time and experience. But, the power women need to acquire capacity to work in groups and to play different roles. They must have constant interface with the outside world—the Government officials, the politicians, civil society institutions and other groups of poor. The groups must acquire the skills of interaction with external environment.

The strategy for empowerment of women must be three-fold:

- Education that promotes building a positive self-image and self-confidence among women and develops their ability to think critically,
- Skill development and employment for economic independence, and
- Increasing awareness among women about health, nutrition, environment, economic and political processes to ensure equal participation in the process of bringing social change.

The empowerment of women is linked with their educational and economic status in the society. Women are in a state of economic, social, political and knowledge disempowerment. The solution lies in reversing this trend and to empowering them socially, economically and politically. This status can be achieved through capacity building facilities like access to education, knowledge, skill development and information.

Agencies of Empowerment

Since Independence, the Government of India (GOI) policies for women's development have evolved in emphasis, from an initial welfare-oriented approach to the current focus on development and empowerment. Significant changes occurred in the mid-1980s with the Seventh Five Year Plan, which operationalize the concern for women's equality and empowerment and focused on inculcating confidence among women, generating awareness of their rights and privileges, training them for economic activity and employment and bringing them into the mainstream of national development.

Within the country especially in third world countries the process of empowerment of poor women is different from that of the middle and the rich class. Poor women must be provided with basic needs, increase in their income, make them literate and involved in skill development to empower them. Changing the patriarchal values, gender division of labour, removal of social seclusion, economic independence, and gender sensitization are more appropriate to empower middle and rich women. Due to poverty, illiteracy and patriarchal values poor women cannot be empowered on their own. The empowerment process through external intervention is inevitable in the third world. Intervention comes through Government, women's movement and Non-Governmental Organizations (NGOs).

In individual empowerment woman must be conscious of herself, her rights, her potentialities, aware of what is happening to her and factors which are acting for and against her. Since it is the woman who is benefited if she is empowered, initiation and demand must come from her regarding what she wants and how to get it.

Empowerment also means having choices and women's ability to make choices. Women must be made to recognize the choices they have, enable them make the choices. Then automatically they will choose their choices on their own. For example, education is one of the choices, women must be made aware of the importance of education and choices in the forms of education available, opportunity must be given and then will make the best use of choices.

Empowerment as an objective of economic development should be a welcome addition to the democratic discourse. After all, oppressed groups ranging from unorganized workers and poor peasants to tribal people, dalits and women have been engaged in a struggle for power and should normally judge the development process in those terms. Whether development projects had led to their appropriations and subjugation was the issue raised by the various movements of displaced people and ecological movements among others.

So, when documents of the UN summits as also the declarations of the national Governments eloquently stress their commitment to empowerment of people, the normal reaction is one of positive glee among the democratic forces. However, the context of the popularization which underlines it make it a questionable concept.

As an illustration, let us take up the documents related to the World Summit for Social Development held in Copenhagen of March 6-12, 1995 where 'empowerment' figures prominently as an objective. The Declaration signed by the heads of the states and Governments says the following: We affirm that in both economic and social terms, the most productive policies and investments are those which empower people to maximize their capacities, resources and opportunities.

The declaration and the Programme of Action have many such statements which clearly link up empowerment with economic globalization. This statement also implies that empowerment as such—even in the sense it is used here—it not the goal, but something to be understood in the context of production and investment. At another place there is a little more focus on empowerment. (Susheela Kaushik). It is to recognize that empowering people particularly women, to strengthen their capacities is a main objective development requires the full participation of people in the formulation of implementation and evaluation of decisions determining the functioning and the well-being of our societies.

There is a certain definition of 'empowerment' suggested in this statement as 'strengthening of capacities' is of course which can be achieved through full participation of people in political process. Strengthening of capacities is of course, crucial to the liberation of oppressed. But, is it possible to achieve that without removing the structural constraints on their capacities? Such definition does not imply liberation from the bondages which have historically constrained fuller realization of human potential in the case of the deprived. Such constrained operated at various levels including socio-economic structure, ideology and political process which the omnibus concept of 'empowerment' does not capture. (Robert S. Lane, 1961). Then there is process of exploitation which encompass the entire society.

Some which afflict several sectors or groups, yet others which target specific classes, castes, ethnic groups and others. Without a relevant disaggregation, the autonomous significance of specific struggles is not acknowledged nor is an appropriate inter-connection established. Hence, strengthening their capacities boils down to an over generalized, albeit noble, statement of intent with little political value to the oppressed.

One of the most important ideological segments of the women movements is the "empowerment", it aims at the political as well as personal empowerment of women in both urban and rural areas. Frequently, it is the educated and middle class urban women who are instrumental in organizing the rural and urban poor women. The largest organizations are headed by educated, urban women with extensive prior experience in politics whose backgrounds are strikingly similar to those of leaders in the right wing.

Their leadership has been the most vital resource in the establishment of empowerment groups; poor, illiterate women do engage in spontaneous protest but cannot sustain an organization without the help of "educated activists". (Susheela Kaushik, 1993). In the empowerment concept there is also a notion of rights, but the goal is economic and social rights—the right to a livelihood and to determine one's own future. The search for empowerment from below not the conferring of rights or economic development from above.

Typically, the organizations mobilize poor women to seek expanded economic opportunity. In rural areas, this may involve an urban area, the creation of small co-operatives, sometimes linked together through a parent organization, is a staple of women Organizations. (Laslie, J. Calman, 1992).

Economic development is just one aim of empowerment. There

is also a self-conscious attempt to create organizational forms in which women become empowered psychologically and socially. Participating in decision-making and in the implementation of women in the family and community; creating mutual inter-dependence and group solidarity; developing skills, self-confidence and secretiveness. All these are seen as integral to the process of empowerment the small local groups that form the grass-roots of these movements foster economic growth, but become more than that. They are support groups that emotionally and intellectually empower, the location of access to local participation as well as the aggregators and articulators of political interests *vis-a-vis* the state (Laslie, J. Calman, 1992).

For a while the empowerment organizations emphasize self-help and the power of the local community, most are not averse to seeking and accepting resources both from international donors (including development agencies such as the Food Foundation, organizations affiliated with the United Nations and bilateral aid from friendly Governments, including several Scandinavian countries and from Findlay Government to assist in organizing or in implementing the economic development schemes they purse). However, some of the empowerment organizations, motivated by a socialist's disdain for the existing parliamentary system and for international capitalism, do not seek any such outside intervention, which they regard as inherently co-operative.

Thus, within those organizations that seek empowerment, a distinction must be drawn between those that view the state as an enemy with which they must inevitably clash, and those that see the state as a potentially and store of resources. To distinguish between the "rights" and "empowerment" will be helpful as a way of marking differences in priorities but, on the ground, the barrier between the two is a fluid one the emphasis is different but not mutually exclusive and often a single organization will engage in both types of activities simultaneously.

Thus, for example, the Women's Wing of the CPM, the all India coordinating committee of working women, not only engages in demonstrations and lobbying aimed at influencing legislation on such "rights" issues as dowry and changes in law regarding Muslim women's right to receive maintenance upon divorce but also organizes working women within the rubric of the CPM sponsored labour union, CITU. Urban "think tanks" such as the centre for Women's Development studies in New Delhi or the Research Centre on Women's Studies of SNDT University in Bombay will provide scholarly support for legal arguments made by groups attempting to influence legislation. They will also sponsor study groups or even entire projects directed at organizing and empowering poor rural women. By the same token, SEWA and Working Women's Forum, as they woke to empower women, continually interact with Government agencies to obtain resources, ease police harassment, or make labour laws responsive to the needs of the self-employed. (Laslie, J. Calman, 1992).

It is the quest for empowerment that most activity as distinct from politics-as-usual within the electoral system. That the women's movements can be seen to be part of a broader set of Indian non-party movements that eschew electoral politics and focus instead on empowering the grass-roots.

Empowerment is multi-dimensional and refers to the expansion of freedom of choice and action in social, economic and political spheres to shape one's life. Since empowerment of women is the key to the socio-economic development of the community, bringing women into the mainstream of national development has been a major concern of the Government and hence has received attention right from the beginning of Indian planning.

However, the shift from "welfare" to "development" of women took place in the Sixth Five Year Plan (1980-85). The Eighth Plan (1992-97) promised to ensure that benefits of development from different sectors do not bypass women. The Ninth Plan (1997-2002) made two significant changes in the strategy of planning for women. Firstly, "empowerment of women" became a primary objective and secondly, the plan attempted "Convergence of existing Services" available in both women-specific and women-related sectors.

The Tenth Plan (2002-07) has made a major commitment towards "empowering women as the agents of socio-economic change and development". Based on the recommendation of National Policy for Empowerment of Women, 2001 the Tenth Plan suggests a three-fold strategy for empowering women, through social empowerment, economic empowerment and gender justice. Gender equality and empowerment of women is recognized globally as a key element to achieve progress in economic sphere. It is one of the eight

Millennium Development goals to which world leaders agreed at the Millennium Summit held in New York in 2000. In India too, a number of women-specific and women-related policies were enunciated.

The National Plan of Action for Women adopted in 1976 became a guiding document for the development of women. A National Perspective Plan for Women (1988-2000) was drafted advocating a holistic approach for the development of women. The National Nutrition Policy, the National Policy on Education and the National Population Policy have significant component for women aimed at their empowerment.

Indian Constitution in its fundamental rights has provisions for equality, social justice and protection of women. These goals are yet to be realized. Still women continue to be discriminated, exploited and exposed to inequalities at various levels. So, the concept of empowerment as a goal of development projects and programmes has been gaining wider acceptance.

By empowerment women would be able to develop self-esteem, confidence, realize their potential and enhance their collective bargaining power. Women empowerment can be viewed as a continuum of several interrelated and mutually reinforcing components (Marilee, Karl, 1995). They are:

- Awareness building about women's situation, discrimination and rights and opportunities as a step towards gender equality. Collective awareness building provides a sense of group identity and the power of working as a group.
- Capacity building and skill development, especially the ability to plan, make decisions, organize, manage and carry out activities to deal with people and institutions in the world around them.
- Participation and greater control and decision-making power in the home, community and society.
- Action to bring about greater equality between men and women.

Thus, empowerment is a process of awareness and capacity building leading to greater participation, greater decision-making power and control and transformative action. The empowerment of women covers both an individual and collective transformation. It strengthens their innate ability through acquiring knowledge, power and experience.

Constitutional guarantees, legislative measures and policies advocating women's concern and presented in the various Ministries, documents namely Women and Child Development, Science and Technology, Ministries namely Health and Family Welfare, Labour, Rural Areas and Employment, Urban Affairs and Employment, Agriculture and Welfare had listed out their programmes and achievements.

The Ninth Plan (1997-2002) had made its commitment to the objective of "empowering women as the agents of social change and development". The twelve salient strategies spelt out focused on empowering women by making women economically independent and self-reliant. It was being hoped that the strategies would be realized through the National Policy for empowerment of women. Remarkably, Self-Help Groups were considered to be one of the strategies to mark the beginning of major process of empowering women.

Committee on the empowerment of women was constituted on April 1997 to improve the status of women. It consisted of 30 members, 20 members of Lok Sabha, 10 members of Rajya Sabha of Indian parliament. The Committee presented its first report on "Developmental Schemes for Rural Women" to Lok Sabha on 21 April 1999. The functions of the Committee included examining the measure to secure women's equality, status and dignity in all matters and considering the reports of National Commission for Women. They also undertook on-the-spot visits in connection with the representatives of elected Panchayat Raj institutions and Municipal bodies.

Planning Commission (1999-2000) had given specific emphasis on empowerment of women, besides the continuation of the important initiative programmes like Rural Women's Development and Empowerment Project (RWDEP) was introduced in the States of Uttar Pradesh, Madhya Pradesh, Bihar, Haryana, Karnataka and Gujarat for a period of five years. The overall objective of the project is to enable empowerment of women by establishing Self-Help Groups which will improve the quality of their lives through greater access to and control over resources.

In order to alter the scenario the year 2001 has been declared as the Year of Women Empowerment and in order to help women focused on issues of importance, each month had a theme on women.

In all the elections held so far in India more than half voters are women, but only a nominal number of them were elected either to the Parliament or Legislative Assemblies. This indicates that votes are from women but victory is for men. The Chinese believe that feudal type of culture does not give new values. Man who had a strong feeling that half of the sky belongs to women and he proved through his theories. Chinese are the first personalities provided the legal right for women on movable and immovable properties.

The women folk got an identity without the husbands influence or so. Moreover they have provided legal right for women to marry the persons whom she likes and at the same time she has the right to give divorce also. The Chinese constitution clearly indicates that women has equal rights along with men in all aspects like political, economical, cultural, social and in family affairs, prevailing of such type of equality in the constitution is not more important, but it's more effective if the Government implements it in right manner. The reason behind the women's development in China is that they not only included in constitution but they have been effectively implemented. In Government of China the women are 30% in employment. In Parliament more than half are deputies. China stood fourth place among the develop countries and 12th in world in providing women in such type of equality. Though the Indian Constitution provides equally rights, it is an irony the less than 10% women Parliamentarians are not present in Parliament of India. (Abhilasha Kumari and Sabina Kidwai, 1998).

In the Panchayati Raj institution and other local bodies the Government has provided one-third's reservations for women for achieving their political empowerment. (Randal Vicky, 1982). It has to be find out better the women has really get benefited by these measures of Government. In this context, Norway's experience can taken as an example. Norway was the idea country the worked provided equal rights in all aspects, like women atrocities, women harassment and discrimination all the political parties in Norway are provided 40% opportunities for them ranking in consideration of women desires, and their abilities. All such things are motivated due to the previous struggles. In 1970, all the political parties provided positions for women in all stages and gave the top priority for women. Through the system came later in providing women equal rights depending upon the ratio of population. It stood behind far the cause. Like people's representation, that is, the reason Norway stood on top in all dimensions.

Indicators of Empowerment

There are several indictors of empowerment. At the individual level participation in crucial decision-making process, ability to prevent violence, self-confidence and self-esteem, improve health and nutrition conditions and at the community level, existence of women's organizations increased number of women leaders, involvement of women in designing development tools and application of appropriate technology, etc. At national level, the indicators are, for example, awareness for her social and political rights, adequate representation in legislative bodies, integrations of women in particular in national development plans, etc. (Medel-Anonueno, 1995)

- Change in women's self-image from one of subordination and subjugation to one of self-esteem, confidence and equality.
- Women's knowledge and awareness of their own situation, social, economic and political forces of health, nutrition, reproductive rights, law, literacy and world around them increased dramatically.
- Formation of articulate cohesive women's group/collectives.
- Formation of formal/in-formal federations/net-works of women's groups who can united engage in struggles and action on common concerns and issues.
- Women's groups collectively access resources/schemes/ services to meet their needs. For example, health, nutrition, child-care, etc.
- Women's ability to speak out and act on oppressive practices and violence against women within the family and outside it.

Understanding that empowerment is a complex issue with varying interpretation in different societal, national and cultural contexts, the participants also came out with a tentative listing of indicators.

At the level of the individual woman and her household Participation in crucial decision-making processes

- Extent of sharing of domestic work by men.
- Extent to which a woman takes control of her reproductive functions and decides on family size.
- Extent to which a woman is able decide where the income she has earned will be chanelled to.
- Felling and expression of pride and value in her work.
- Self-confidence and self-esteem.
- Ability to prevent violence.

At the community and or organisational-level Existence of women's organisations

- Allocation of funds to women and women's projects.
- Increased number of women leaders at village, district, provincial and national-levels.
- Involvement of women in the design, development and application of technology.
- Participation in community programmes, productive enterprises, politics and arts.
- Involvement of women in non-traditional tasks.
- Increased training programmes for women.
- Exercising her legal rights when necessary.

At the National-level

- Awareness of her social and political rights.
- Integration of women in the general national development plan.
- Existence of women's networks and publications.
- Extent to which women are officially visible and recognized.
- The degree to which the media take need of women's issues.

Facilitating and Constraining Factors of Empowerment

Empowerment does not take place in a vacuum. In the same way that Ms. Lazo talks about women's state of powerlessness as a result of "a combination and interaction of environmental factors", one can also discuss the condition or factors that can hasten or hinder empowerment. As above, the listing is a preliminary one based on the discussions.

Facilitating Factors

- Existence of women's organisation.
- Availability of support systems for women,
- Availability of women—specific data and other relevant information.
- Availability of funds.
- Feminist leadership.
- Networking.
- Favourable media coverage.
- Favourable policy climate.

Constraining Factors

- Heavy work load of women.
- Isolation of women each other.
- Illiteracy.
- Traditional views that limit women's participation.
- No funds.
- Internal strife or militarization or wars.
- Disagreements or conflicts among women's groups.
- Structural adjustment policies.
- Discriminatory policy environment.
- Negative and sensational coverage of media.

Creating Empowerment

The prime target of empowerment must be adult women and in the context of social justice and transformation, they must be low-income adult women. Within this group, authoritarian behaviours by husbands in the home make families and households in general a terrain that serves the maintenance rather the transformation of unequal gender relations.

A pre-requisite to empowerment, necessitates stepping outside the home and participating in some form of collective undertaking that can be successful, thus developing a sense of independence and competence among the women. The creation of a small, cohesive group, with which its members may identify closely is paramount. We know that because of the small scale and voluntary nature of these associations many members gain valuable experience and confidence in both leadership and membership tasks. The central activity of the group could vary; it could be literacy activity, income-generation, mutual basic needs support, etc. Whatever the objective, the group activity should be designed so that its process and its goal-attainment foster the development of a sense of self-esteem, competence and autonomy.

Empowerment will go through a series of phase. Awareness of conditions at the personal and collective levels will lead to some public action, however small. Following from this beginning there should occur a re-negotiation of family conditions. As women become more available for public action, they should be able to place more demands upon the state.

Women can attain empowerment through different points of departure: emancipatory knowledge, economic leverage, political mobilization. While many poor women work outside the home to support their families and the tasks they perform are exhausting and meagerly rewarded, access to income improves their authority in the home. Working women, regardless of how inferior their position and small their income, have a greater sense of control over their lives and more power and control resources within the family than networking women.

Significance of Women Empowerment

The term 'empowerment' has gained significance and prominence recently among policy makers and researchers. In the field of women's studies and social work it is viewed with a holistic perspective and it can be classified as social, educational, economical, political and psychological empowerment. To quote Thomas and Pierson, empowerment referred to user participation in services and to the self-help movement generally, in which groups took action on their own behalf, either in cooperation with or independently of the statutory services. Empowerment is concerned with how people may gain collective control over their lives, so as to achieve their interests as a group and a method by which social workers seek to enhance the power of people who lack it.

The empowerment of women would create a new world of equality between men and women. It should remove the subordination of women. Once they become empowered, they can have control over their labour, income, sexuality, reproduction and mobility. They will not accept the existing stereotyped roles, gender division of labour, and any other beliefs or systems, which are oppressive.

Empowered women "instead of remaining silent and unquestioning they become articulate and questioned they become educated from uneducated, changed gender division, labour instead of accepting blindly, they got free mobility in the place of restricted mobility". (Srilatha Batliwala, 1995).

In the process of empowerment they become economically independent not only in earning but also in having control over their income. They would be able to face problems in the life either individually or collectively. They can socialize their children and make them more gender sensitive. They would be able to get a global view of their issues, which had limited view, by making personal issue a political issue. If power is defined as 'power over', a gender analysis shows that power is wielded predominantly by men over other men, and by men over women. If women gain power, it will be at men's expenses. There might be inherent threat due to some kind of reversal of relationships by which men will not only lose power but also face the possibility of having power wielded over them by women. Men's fear of losing control is an obstacle to women's empowerment. In this context of 'power over' women should be empowered participate within the economic and political structure of society, whereas 'power to' refers to increasing one's ability to resist and challenge 'power over'. (Jo Rowland, 1997).

The process of empowerment cannot take place all of a sudden. It pass through various stages, like in the first stage women try to look into the situation from a different perspective, recognize the power structure and other institutional norms which subordinate them by keeping themselves away from them. In this stage, they also try to share their feelings and experiences with other women and realize that is not single women's experience but common to all.

In the second stage, they try to change the situation, and structure which are against them. They not only point out the injustice done to them but also resist them. Here they got support and strength from collective action.

In the third stage, they become more mature and realize that what they are and how they are is not their fate but it is imposed on them, they lack something and they have to gain it, for that they need to know more, learn more and work more. With the collective work they cultivate confidence upon themselves.

Collective empowerment of women would shift the direction and process of development to women's needs and their demand. It would bring with it the individual empowerment of women not merely for individual advancement but for the advancement of society as a whole. Empowerment may also bring negative impacts. It would bring conflict between men and women while changing the gender relation. Men will have to loose something, which they are having and enjoying since a long time. So, in the process of empowerment if women gain something, men have to loose something.

Empowerment of women may result in the emergence of single big mass group to protect the democratic values, to fight against the social evils, to fight for social justice, to work for the cause of all those who are deprived of it. But, the way of empowerment is not free from hurdles. Patriarchal norms, traditional beliefs, economic system, political conditions make the task of empowering women more complicated. Since, patriarchy is found to be very deeply entrenched both in men and women empowering women has become an extremely complex task. Achieving gender equality and changing the present gender relations requires widespread changes in the thinking and structure of every institution of changes in the society. Women empowerment can only be achieved through integrated and synergetic thinking and action. (Kamala Bhasin and Sunnita Dhar, 1995)

While empowering women an effort may be biased in favour of women. But, empowerment implies a positive role and participation of women in national development not only their own behalf but for the benefit of society at large. Empowerment of women enhances their ability to make choices within the family and in the society.

Empowerment is wider sense benefit not only women themselves but also the family, the economy and the society. So, it recognized in the HDR 1995 that "empowering people—particularly women is a sure way to link growth and human development". (Human Development Report, 1995).

Empowerment is a process and is not, therefore, something that can be given to people. The process of empowerment is both individual and collective, since it is through involvement in groups that people most often begin to develop their awareness and the ability to organize to take action and bring about change. Women empowerment can be viewed as a continuum of several interrelated and mutually reinforcing components:

- Awareness building about women's situation, discrimination, and rights opportunities as a step towards gender equality. Collective awareness building provides a sense of group identify and the power of working as a group.
- Capacity building and skills development, especially the ability to plan, make decisions, organize, manage and carry out activities, to deal with people and institutions in the world around them.
- Participation and greater control and decision-making power in the home, community and society.
- Action to bring about greater equality between men and women.

In short, empowerment is a process of awareness and capacity building leading to greater participation, to greater decision-making power and control, and to transformative action.

SPHERES OF WOMEN EMPOWERMENT

Women of the world should be empowered to take control of all spheres of their lives—academically, economically, socially and politically.

Academic

- Instead of being compressed into the domestic sphere, and looked upon as unpaid servant and a biological machine for bearing and rearing children, every girl child and woman should have an access to education. Women's education is indispensable as all feminists unanimously view that women empowerment and realization of her rights can be achieved only through education.
- Awareness can be generated among the masses through conduct of a series of Seminars, Workshops, Symposia, covering a broad spectrum of womenfolk belonging to all

strata of life. This will ensure that the fight against violation of human rights grows into people's movement. Similarly, the human rights day should be celebrated as a consciousness—raising day to sensitize individuals of all ages about their rights.

- Educational institutions can play a vital role in dissemination of human rights through periodic conduct of several competitions, such as, quiz, essay writing, oration, painting, photographs, cartoons, etc. The student community should be encouraged to express their views in both regional and national languages.

Economic

- Effective measure should be taken to alleviate poverty, as poverty is one of the crucial violations of human rights. Food security is one of the basic human rights of every individual, hence this should be assured at all cause. A majority of girl children and women suffer from low nutritional status owing to the presence of intra-household gender discrimination in food distribution, which should be eliminated through a proper sensitization of women on gender equality.
- Women should have an equal access to institutional credit. Loan facilities for women can be expanded through formation of co-operative credit societies, as this would promote self-employment and entrepreneurship among women.
- Training and skill formation is necessary to enable women to liberate themselves from unskilled, low paid works of agriculture, construction, domestic work, etc.
- Women should be ensured equal wages for equal work. Employment laws relating to maternity benefits, prohibition of women in hazardous works, provision of crèche facilities, old age pension, etc. should be extended to cover women employed in the informal sectors who are at present deprived of these benefits.
- The rights of a child to education can be achieved only if there is total ban on child labour, which still persists despite all Governmental measures aimed at removing child labour.

Socio-Cultural

- ❖ Women should be made aware of their rights relating to rape, dowry, female infanticide, wife beating and other forms of violence against women. This awareness can be created through the media and Non-Governmental Organizations.
- ❖ Despite all Governmental measures, violence against women in escalating, which can be curbed and tackled effectively through setting up of Human Rights Cell at all District Headquarters, which should be linked with small women's forums/groups functioning at the village level, so that realistic details can be gathered and redressal measures can be enacted immediately.
- ❖ Paralleling that of Gandhi's Ahimsa, a movement of human rights should take place, encompassing every woman, belonging to diverse background, within its fold. This movement must touch every woman's lie, educate her about her rights, teach her to assist herself to have control over her reproductive capacity, mostly that she has a right to order her life first.
- ❖ Women being deprived of their rights in the names of customs, religious practices, values and traditions must be stopped through attitudinal changes and value education.
- ❖ Women's right to health care should be recognized as an important factor and an easy and accessible health care should be made available particularly for the rural and tribal women as these groups of women are gone to high rate of maternal deaths.

Political

- ❖ There should be 50 per cent representation of women in the Parliament, State assemblies and Local Self-Governments. In all committees relating to all aspects of human rights, at least one-third should be headed by women.
- ❖ A special training programme for women should be undertaken for their effective participation in politics, since most women are ignorant and shy away from politics.
- ❖ A special monitoring and enforcement agency should be formulated at the District-levels, with members constituting of women's organizations, Non-Governmental

Organizations, Government and academic bodies, to review and assess the crimes against women.

- Human rights training are to be given to paramilitary forces and police personnel for protection of human rights particularly for women in their custody.
- Ethnic clashes are the order of the day which is a threat to the personal security of every individual. No amount of legal and other measures can stem this violation of human rights unless there is transformation in every individual along with humanitarian concern and care for the life of another human being.

Legal

- There should be a provision for setting up special human rights court in each District for "speedy trial" of offences arising out of violation of human rights.
- The setting up of two Commissions in India—the National Human Rights Commission and the National Commission for Women in 1993, is a positive step, but their area of operation is limited and they lack the expected enforcement for which they were designed.
- Right to a healthy environment is now being acknowledged as one of the fundamental human rights, as environmental degradation is responsible for deteriorating health status of people and hence deter sustainable human development.

A significant step in the political empowerment of women was the constitutional amendments of 73 and 74 of 1993, which provided for the reservation of 1/3 of the total seats for women in local bodies in both rural and urban areas. Andhra Pradesh is one of the pioneering states, which implemented the rule of reservation not only in the local bodies but also in the Government jobs as well as in the admission in the schools and colleges. The Bill, providing reservation of 1/3 of seats in the Legislative Assemblies and Parliament has been introduced recently in Parliament, yet the consensus has not been arrived.

Empowerment is a goal, a strategy and a process. It is a combination of both. It is a process of action and reflection. It can generate new notions of power. Empowerment is a collective action.

Empowerment as a concept was introduced at the International Women's Conference in 1985 at Nairobi. The Conference defined empowerment as a redistribution of social power and control of resources in favour of women. In the true sense of the word, empowerment would mean giving-up old established ways, habits and giving-up privileges.

The programme of action 1992 has comprehensively given the below mentioned parameters of empowerment of women:

- Enhance self-esteem and self-confidence in women.
- Build a positive image of women by recognizing their contribution to the society, polity and economy.
- Develop them an ability to think critically.
- Foster decision-making and action through collective process.
- Enable women to make informed choices in areas like education, employment and health especially reproductive health.
- Ensure equal participation in the developmental process.
- Provide information, knowledge and skill for economic independence.
- Enhance access to legal literacy and information related to their rights and entitlements in the society with a view to enhance their participation on an equal footing in all areas.

The subordinate position of women has many manifestations in the society. The limited representation of women in the formal political system, the presence of large number of women in the informal sector with reduced financial rewards, the near exclusive responsibilities for family and children, low level of aspiration and low self-esteem are some of the important manifestations of women's subordinate position. The subordination of women has many facets so also the empowerment of women. Empowerment is a socio-political concept and goes beyond the formal political participation and awareness among women.

Empowerment of women involves clear and well-defined strategies. Creation of women's organization is the key to the empowerment process. In the present situation, the adult women from low-income group should be given more preference. The reasons for this preference are not far to seek. The adult women in the low-income group are severely affected by the authoritarian behaviour of men. The households of low income group functions as a system that maintains unequal gender relationship.

Hence, adult women from lower income group should be given preference in the empowerment process. The first step of empowerment process is the women to step out of the home and participate in some form of collective understanding. This can develop a sense of independence and competence among women. The creation of a small, cohesive group with which its members can identify very closely is important. This small and voluntary nature of these associations will give valuable experience for women in leadership and membership tasks. The group activities should be designed in such a way to foster a sense of self-esteem, competence and autonomy among its members. There are a number of ways to empower women.

A most debated concept and elaborately discussed issue of recent years is women empowerment. Seminars, conferences, workshops and a number of meetings are organized to discuss in depth on the strategies and modus operandi towards achieving women empowerment more than clarifying it conceptually. Women empowerment is considered as a goal hence necessary aspects of such a goal are investigated at all levels especially in the context of policy-making and project formulation in view of developing women in the country. The latest attempt of the government of India to introduce Women Empowerment Bill of 2001 reflects undoubtedly the necessity of achieving it as goal. A nineteen paged policy document contains all issues pertaining to women, all possible strategies are fixed and targets are determined, with a belief that such measures would ultimately 'empower', i.e. facilitate women empowerment in the country.

Women empowerment is perhaps a vital component for reaching gender equality, hence, refers to equitable access to resource, power and decision-making. Aspects like women's development, performance, skill acquisition, participation in policy-decision all make women empowerment a positive concept. Feminists refer it to women's capacity for self-action, power to change their course of life and also to adapt to the challenges in time. It is viewed as a process that requires a realignment of power in decision-making at all levels *vis-a-vis* household, personal, institutional and social levels.

Women empowerment is a multi-dimensional process, aiming at establishing an equitable partnership between men and women that can be built on the strengths of shared living: in terms of knowledge, energy, creativity and skill. Equitable partnership—a state of empowerment—becomes vital as it is perceived to bring positive benefits to the society and solutions to global problems, that are pressing the world's economy, environment and social living. Women empowerment as such is viewed to facilitate a joint venture of men and women in combating the global problems.

International Scenario on Women Empowerment

There had been women's conferences held at the international level. One in Mexico in 1975 and another in Copenhagen in 1980, yet another in Nairobi in 1985 and the recent one was in Beijing in September 1995, that includes an NGO forum in Huairou. Discussions interacted during such conferences revealed the potentials of women's movements at the international level in maximizing advocacy efforts towards empowering women worldwide:

- In creating constituencies free from male dominated governments,
- In establishing a new government, sought to be influenced by women, Subsequent conferences of the United Nations held in Riode, Janeiva, Vienna, Cairo, Small Islands, Copenhagen and Habitat II paved way for multiplying international contact and networking among women,
- In all these conferences, the key issues affecting women world-wide were identified,
- Women's economic survival,
- Global economy,
- Empowerment of women,
- Poverty,
- Affordable health care,
- Human rights,
- Workplace rights,
- Educational equity,
- Reproductive and sexual rights,
- Struggles against violence, and
- Protection of healthy environment and end to wars and militarism.

Beijing Declaration on Women Empowerment

The largest United Nation's conference the world is said to have seen, was the United Nation's Fourth World Conference of Women held in Beijing. It was reported as a consensus of official representatives from 189 countries and 30,000 NGO representatives consisting of 20,000 women and the rest being men, which manifested the power of women as force for global change towards developing countries and benefiting the human kind. The desired goal of the conference was gender equality, which could be achieved by mainstreaming perspective in development process.

Feminists acknowledged that Beijing conference spoke of many things, but emphasized categorically on paradigm shifts, women empowerment and the male-female relationship. The need for considering these things was stressed not as somebody's business but as everybody's business. The success of the conference was in its contribution towards a change of mindset in people all over the world.

Of course, the seed for women empowerment was sown even earlier at the International Conference on Population and development held in Cairo, in 1994. Women representatives from all over the countries contorted over the population policies that remain still abusive to women and declared recognizing the centrality of women empowerment both in the population policy and in development policy. Thus, women empowerment received the first attention in the priority list along with gender equality, women's ability to control their own fertility and elimination of violence against women. Such a view was also endorsed in Beijing declaration, that states "We, the governments' participating in the Fourth World Conference on Women, dedicate ourselves unreservedly to addressing the constraints and obstacles empowerment of women all over the world and agree that this requires urgent action in the spirit of determination, hope, co-operation and solidarity now and to carry us forward into next century".

The agenda for women empowerment named as the platform for actions, prepared unanimously at the Beijing conference seeks to promote and protect the full enjoyment of all human rights and the fundamental freedom for all women throughout their life. This agenda called for establishing the principle of shared power and responsibility between women and men at home, at workplace and at the level of wider national and international communities. Thus, women empowerment is conceived to be the whole bundle of women's rights *vis-a-vis* to freedom of thought, consciences, religion, and belief, intending to contribute to the moral, ethical, spiritual and intellectual needs of women and men as at the personal or communal spheres.

Women's Concerns in the Context of Empowerment

The critical areas of women's concern have been identified at the fifth Regional Conference on Women held in Africa. They are: women's:

- Poverty,
- Insufficient food security and lack of economic opportunities,
- Inadequate access to education, training, science and technology,
- Vital role in culture, family and socialization,
- Improvement of health in general and reproductive health in particular,
- Relationship and linkages to environment and natural resources management,
- Involvement in peace process,
- Political participation,
- Legal and human rights, and
- Mainstreaming gender disegregated data as well as the status of girl child.

Women empowerment is closely tied with health and education guaranteeing them the possibility of realizing their full potentials in society, and shaping their lives concomitant to their aspirations. It is thus a fundamental factor for achieving equality, development and peace in the country, ultimately leading to full participation of women in all spheres i.e., decision-making process and access to power.

Empowerment Framework

Empowerment need to be treated both as a process and as a goal, indicating the fact that it is an end by itself and a means as well, to reach this ultimate. Similar to socialization, empowerment takes women to the extent that they think and act self-decisively. It becomes as stage of self-thinking, self-acting, self-made and self-decisive in all walks of life with a positive role performance and role-fulfilment. At this stage the role and statuses of women and men become common, equal and jointly ventured aspirations and ambitions. There will not be stereotyped, sex-based division of labour, rather-merit-based, skill-based allocation of tasks. Rewards and punishments are geared towards the skillful performance of the individuals rather than on the sex of the individuals. Societies particularly the governance aims at reaching that state of affairs through women empowerment.

When empowerment is treated as a goal, then there are steps to reach the goal, which is explained as empowerment framework. Empowerment framework is found inclusive of five major stages or Levels of equality, such as Welfare, Access, Concretization, Participation, and Control. Each stage advances further into the next, one finally resulting at empowered stage. (Sahay Sushama, 1998)

Welfare

Welfare is the first and foremost stage, in which the governance address to the basic needs of women, such as economic, health, nutrition, legal, psychological and social. Obviously the role of State is greatly required to formulate welfare policies and plan for welfare programmes to be implemented. The privileges, provisions, concessions, assistance and other services of the State, are being utilized by women. Women at this stage remain as passive recipients and beneficiaries of the target groups. As a consequence, the governance attempts to identify the problems of women like poverty, literacy, poor health and malnutrition, backwardness, etc. presented in term of statistical demographic, health and other data documents. Targeted women categories become beneficiaries of these programmes without addressing to the cause and consequence of their problems and the redressals respectively. However, welfare measures do form an important component of empowerment framework. Perhaps it is the stepping stone for women to be empowered.

Access

Access is following welfare because all the welfare services made available to them, must be practically accessible to women for use.

It is the effort of governance to make the resource accessible to women especially in the field of education, health, media, employment, land credit, marketing, administration, training and other opportunities. For example, every village is supplied with a television, kept in the community hall, under the lack and key and under the custody of somebody like the village president. Women are not allowed to view television as and when they like to use it.

Similarly, agricultural trainings given to women on the application of fertilizers or pesticides on the paddy/cultivable land, that does not belong to them as the land is in possession of some male member in the family. These are typical contexts of availability of resource but not being accessible to women. Thus, women should become accessible to resources, in this second stage, where women and resources are to be brought closer to each other.

Concretization

Concretization is crucial stage, in that women are exposed not only to realize their problems, interest, needs requirements but also to recognize the causes, consequences, remedial measure to end those problems. Especially the structural and institutional arrangements of the society to have caused their problems is made known to women. For example, women might come to know that the traditional roles of the society have not only domesticated them but also restricted women's growth and progress outside home. Hence, in this stage, all women are involved in the process of consciousness-raising, but which they develop feminist consciousness from themselves. Awareness camps tend to awaken women by arousing their 'we-feeling' and mobilize them towards achieving their cause.

Participation

A woman, raised with consciousness about her role and status comes to realize her contribution and importance in the society, that motivate her to participate in all spheres. In this stage, women, not only think and decide by themselves, but also initiate performance and fulfil their aspirations with respect to literacy, employment, and public life. Thereby they begin to mobilize themselves and carry out activities in an organized way, thus work collectively for the cause of women. Formation of women collectives, women organization, emerging women leadership in public life, etc., are nothing but participatory stage of women empowerment.

Control

Control is the ultimate stage of equality otherwise to be viewed as empowered stage. The end product of all the three stages of this process can be realized in the form of goal-setting, formulation of policies pertaining to women's issues, framing women development programmes devising strategies for implementation and preparing a plan of action for their own benefits, so as fulfil their interest in every walk of life at the social level. As a consequence, at the individual level. Women begin to take decisions over`their own lives, children environment and living atmosphere. Women gain control over all matters pertaining to them which develops a balance between men and women as equals. Neither of the gender dominates the other and women's contributions will be duly recognized, valued and be rewarded wherever in the society.

Implications of Women Empowerment

Women empowerment implies a lot of socio-cultural, economic and psychological changes in women both as individuals and as collectives. It signifies fundamentally a change process in women perhaps begins from letting female consciousness out to that of acquiring feminist consciousness. Female consciousness, according to Nannerol keohane is the deep-rooted age old experiences of women in giving and preserving life, nurturing and sustaining, considering women as close to nature i.e., self-image of women as life givers and sustainers. Whereas feminist consciousness is that which is developed and defined as women reflecting on women's experiences, envisaging an alternative way of living without restraints imposed by rigid and impersonal sex roles. In this process, women undergo a lot of change in their psyche, personality and in role-performance. Women empowerment, hence signifies a lot of changes on the following lines according to Kamala Bhasin:

1. Women are being helped to fight their own fears, feeling of inadequacy and inferiority;
2. They are enabled to enhance their self-respect and self-dignity also to control their own bodies;
3. They are prepared to be economically independent and self-reliant;
4. They are made accessible to land, property and other resources;

5. Women's burden of work in domestic chores is considered;
6. Women's contributions and knowledge are being recognized;
7. Women groups and organizations are created and strengthened; and
8. Qualities of new outlook and approach are promoted in women.

Thus empowering women starts with individuals and ends with women collectives, resulting in an ultimate stage of gender equality in the society. Social institutions free from sexist approaches get converted into non-sexist structures, placing men and women on parallel points in the social continuum. As a multidimensional process, empowerment of women includes personal, social and political power, referring to women's capacity for self-action and the power to change the course of their life. Women are helped to build a positive self-image especially to develop basic respect and dignity as capable individuals in their work at the personal level.

At the societal level, attitudinal changes take place in women for which consciousness raising campaigns/camps are organized and public opinions are generated in view of eliminating social ostracism of women of weaker and deprived sections. Social Empowerment of women is also made by organizing remarriage of young widows, separated, divorcees and destitute, also.... Dowry free, non-luxurious marriages. In addition, supportive services to employed women and alternative vocational skill trainings to girl drop-outs and discontinued adult women, health education to poor and prostitutes, extended with rehabilitative measures, are to be provided.

Empowerment of women at the economic sphere, includes employment opportunities to women in organized and unorganized sectors. Women's involvement in trade union activities, formations of thrift societies through self-help group activities, extending credit and marketing facilities, making available land, water and other productive resources to be accessible to women, all empower women economically. Political empowerment of women is possible only through equitable women representative in Parliament, Assemblies and also in Local Self-governance. Women become legally empowered through legal literacy camps, awareness camps on women legal rights, family and legal counseling.

Structural and Institutional Rearrangements Towards Women Empowerment

Scenario of women empowerment has undergone a lot of changes, ranging from the most oppressing to the just liberating stage in India. There are historical evidences to show that the medieval ages right from 8th to 18th century AD had witnessed a most obscure and hazy picture of women. P.N. Pandey narrates it by saying that "it is perhaps the darkest period of Indian womanhood where she was subjected to all sorts of tyranny, oppression, atrocity, exploitations, and the customs like sati, thugi, devadasi, dowry, child marriage, hypergamous marriage, polygenic and restrictions to widow remarriage, and uprooted the dignity and decency of Indian womanhood. The socio-cultural samaj, Brahmo Samaj, Theosophical society attempted to annihilate those social atrocities on women during 19th century. But today perhaps the age old problems of women are removed socially and legally, yet another dimension of atrocities continue to exist. Incidences of rape, wife batterings, dowry harassment/death/murder, female infanticide, abduction, inducement to prostitution, etc., are high and are enhancing so fast indicating the perpetuation of gender inequality and injustice and the persisting problems of women. Changing such a scenario is the crucial and critical task of today's society in India.

Women's education, employment and independent economic status are of course the influential factors for women empowerment. Kuntal Agarwal opines that, "A positive attitude of family member and women's own positive attitude towards themselves is more important for changing women's status towards empowerment. Unfortunately it is lacking, yet it can best be developed by following human and spiritual values in life by all which will help in developing congenial social climate for empowering women". However, women's position has undergone a significant change especially in post-independent India. Most probingly, the theory according to Maharajan that women's range of occupations, were discredited after the two world wars. Thousands of women voluntarily entered industry, agriculture, substituting men, handling machines and taking part in many new tasks in heavy industries including metal, engineering trades and development, their problems are perpetuated, of course in a different dimension. Today, women in India are the victims of rape, dowry, female infanticide, wife battering, revolving around one social institution i.e., family. How are women going to encounter such a situation? Women are ambivalent about the direction of change and strategies for the rural empowerment.

Women empowerment is thus closely associated with effective changes in all social institutions *vis-a-vis* family, marriage, religion, economy, education, polity, etc. Sadiq A. Jilani Syed presents strategies for bringing out social change in view of achieving protection and empowerment of women in general and Muslim women in particular. They consist of "changes in legislation and awareness". Hence, the role of all social institutions like in bringing out an empowered stage of women's life. Generally, it is felt by feminists like Kamala Nath that the paternalistic family and male dominated political structures do not provide space for women in participating in decision-making bodies and process.

Empowerment of women is thus a net result of changes in all the institutions concomitantly and not merely due to changes in any one or two of social institutions. As a continuous process, empowerment needs an art to form a group of women, whose efforts have to be mobilized so as to overcome a lot of obstacles that they face in their day-to-day life. S. Pandi views that women can phase the challenge of life with the principles and ideology of self-help formation only by means of empowerment. The following topology would facilitate the direction with which all strategies would achieve women empowerment in the long run:

> Women empowerment is a continuous and simultaneous process that initiates awareness of the situation and of their problems, a change in their mindset and attitudes of both men and women. Every social institution should initiate a change by providing space of women to voice their interests. Women's questions must be accommodated in all spheres of developmental discussions and debates. It is in this situation of empowerment process, a woman becomes aware of where she is understands why she is in that situation, then gets motivated to change it with her own efforts, seizes the opportunities, decides what she wants and chooses her own future..., says Mayox. Thus, a overall change in the social institutions facilitates change in the attitudes of men in general and women in particular. An empowered woman would strive to break sex-

based stereotypes, questions male domination and superiority, becomes knowledged, skilled, capable and be informative in all aspects of life as equal 'partners'. Ultimately, it is the rights of women that enables them to act, followed after thinking, deciding, choosing, consenting in such a way as to attain equality and fulfil their ambitions and aspirations.

This view has been endorsed by Kamala Nath who perceives the issue of women empowerment as central to the achievement of goals: equality, development and peace i.e., the Beijing declaration. It is essential that women occupy in decision-making positions, as it will ensure the restructuring of institutions that are responsible for women's health. Sexual harassment and other issues as top-priority. Women empowerment is an end by itself and it is also a means to achieve gender equality.

Hence, necessary structural institutional arrangements must be made for initiating women empowerment which in turn pave way for a new structure and institution built on gender equality. At present women's entry to all fields has broken the masculinity of occupations and also the monopoly of men in such occupations and economy. Women in these areas of employment and economy may be less in number and be unproportionate to the total women population, yet they become 'role-models' to a vast majority of women, through their achievements. The real empowerment of women is possible definitely in near future if there are:

- Intensive awareness camps on legal rights conducted among women;
- Skill training and vocational trainings provided to drop-outs and adult women;
- Legislative amendments guaranteeing women to think and act independently especially on social causes, social evils and social problems affecting them so long;
- Women collectives are formed and mobilized;
- Mass women's movements demanding the State to provide reservation in all spheres like education, employment and in politics; and
- The counter-parts perceive correctly women's interests and women's questions.

All these are possible only if childhood socialization becomes effective in imparting a new culture that preaches and practices gender equality. Gender justice and gender development. Family is thus the crux of socialization as well as empowerment processes. Noeleen Heyser, Director of the UNICEM has brought out four important components of women empowerment. They are:

(a) A woman sense of worth;
(b) Woman's right to determine her own choices;
(c) Power to control their own lives within and outside home; and
(d) Her ability to influence the direction of social change and to create a just social and economic order nationally and internationally.

A woman is said to be empowered only when she exercise her own rights and powers without the intrusion of any other members of the family/occupation particularly of the opposite sex namely, the man. The moment she acquires all abilities in such a way that have enabled her to exercises these rights and powers, she is empowered. Thus, the above are not only components but also the indicators of empowerment in women. Necessary skills, psychological approaches, motivation, exposure, training, awareness and awakening, leadership traits, etc. have to be given to women with the ultimate aim of empowering them to be self-reliant, self-dependent, self-sufficient, self-contented, self-achieved and self-satisfied.

The participation of women is a means to achieve the goals of development, through gender-aware, more efficient, economy-wide policies. It will contribute to achieving economic goals, such as economic growth, but it will also help identify the social goals the society is willing to pursue. Indeed, an idea which is gaining momentum is that increased participation of women in decision-making at all levels will help to 'adjust' the goals pursued through development.

As the above statement by the Secretary-General of the United Nations indicates, women's participation is not only essential to economic development; it will also have a transformative effect on the goals of both economic and social development. Women's participation, thus, does not mean simply increasing women's numbers or integrating them into existing development models;

rather, it is part of the process of empowerment and a way to make development policies and programmes more people-centred.

Before the United Nations Decade for Women (1976-85), development policies and programmes were considered to be gender-neutral: that is, they did nor distinguish between men and women but were assumed to benefit automatically all people, women as well as men. Attention was given to women primarily as mothers and carers, or as a particularly 'vulnerable' group. Consequently, programmes directed at women were related mainly to nutrition, child care, health and population, and at improving family life and controlling women's fertility. The programmes were welfare-oriented, designed to help women who were suffering from the worst ravages of poverty and malnutrition. Women's roles in agricultural and other forms of production went unperceived.

Beginning with Easter Boserup, whose ground-breaking book, women's role in economic development, was published in 1970, women researchers and activists began to make women visible as active participants in production, in the household and other sectors of the society. Studies revealed that women have often been victims of development programmes rather than beneficiaries, that many development programmes that were assumed to benefit everybody really benefited men only and often had negative effects not only on women but on the whole community. The high rate of failure of development policies, programmes and projects is attributable at least in part to the neglect or lack of knowledge of women's productive and reproductive roles.

Mainstreaming Women

The unintended marginalization of women in development programmes, projects, and units led development agencies to rethink women in development approaches in the 1980s and to develop new arguments emphasizing the need to mainstream women: that is, to bring women from the margins into the centre of the main development programmes and of the institutions that deal with the economy.

While agreeing that women need to be central to development programmes, some women raised concerns about the consequences of mainstreaming. Does mainstreaming women mean that development agencies no longer need to give attention to the special concerns of women? Would mainstreaming cut-off support to the growing number of women's groups, organizations and network? And is mainstreaming just a new name for integrating women in development? There was also a fear that by jumping into the mainstream women would run the risk of drowning in a male-dominated and male-defined development agenda. Would the interest in women and the large body of research generated in the past two decades ensure women a permanent place on the agenda? In this view, mainstreaming must mean both increasing women's participation in development programmes and ensuring that women's perspectives, needs and concerns constitute the basis of the redefinition of development itself.

Gender and Development

The shift from the integration of women to mainstreaming since the mid-1980s has been accompanied by the shift in focus from women to gender. In contrast to the WID approach, this new approach is generally referred to as Gender and Development (GAD)—Gender is here understood as the socially defined and constructed roles of men and women. Unlike sex, which is biologically determined, gender roles change from one place and culture to another and across time. For example, in nineteenth-century Europe it was considered that only men were suited for office work, whereas by the mid-twentieth century, secretarial work in offices was considered a female occupation. The twentieth century has seen rapid changes in many places in what are considered male and female roles. The focus on gender looks at the roles and needs of both women and men and at how these are interrelated, and thus lessons the risk of marginalizing women.

There are some who see the GAD approach as having the potential to bring in women's visions of development. The Canadian Council for International Cooperation states:

> Gender and Development is emerging as a progressive approach to development from women's perspectives and experiences. It is part of the larger work of creating on alternative development model, for a world view which moves beyond an econometric analysis to include environmental, sustainable and qualitative (personal, ethical and cultural) aspects in its definition of development.

The GAD approach, however, like that of WID, does not in itself question the prevailing development paradigm. Its potential to do so depends on how it is interpreted and applied.

Mainstreaming and Gender Planning Strategies

A number of strategies have been developed to bring women into the mainstream and to make gender a central focus of development programmes. These include:

- strengthening women's units, groups and organizations to ensure gender awareness, to act as pressure groups and to monitor the implementation of mainstreaming women;
- gender awareness and analysis training;
- building a critical mass of women inside development organizations; and
- lobbying and pressuring development institutions.

Although sometimes regarded as contrasting with each other, the strategies are complementary and can be applied in mutually interactive combinations. A mass of women inside development institutions supporting and supported by strong women's non-governmental organizations and research groups can bring pressure to bear on policy-makers and create a climate for gender awareness and analysis. The combination of strategies can enable women to participate in the mainstream and to empower themselves to determine the nature and goals of their participation. Openness to dialogue, collaboration, coalition building and co-ordination are the keys to success.

3

Self-Help Group and Women Empowerment

- Women Empowerment
- Need for Women Empowerment
- Framework for Empowerment
- Components of Empowerment
- Policy Approaches to Third World Women
- National Policy for the Empowerment of Women, 2001
- Great Personalities on Women Empowerment
- Self-Help Groups: As a Movement
- Social Impact and Empowerment of Women

WOMEN EMPOWERMENT

Women empowerment is a global issue and an important concept widely used in multi-dimensional process which enables women to realise and exercise their full identity and powers in all spheres of life. Women form nearly half of the human capital in the country, but they remain the most deprived and long neglected segment of the society, despite the constitutional guarantee for equal rights and privileges for men and women. The marginalization of women in developing societies cannot overcome without examining the roots of marginalization which is the patriarchal system. When development excludes women from full participation, it denies its benefits to women and it functions far less effectively. Changing the mind sets and educating men and women has been a Herculean task. Attitudes and values based on socialization and patriarchal ideology lead us towards a world of inequalibrium. Creation of awareness on women's issues would go a long way in bringing women empowerment which includes the enhancement in the self-confidence of women, better use of their potential and gaining of self control of their lives. This would lead to true development. True development cannot happen when the needs, talents and potentialities of half of the world's population are seen as secondary and marginal. Women's access are restricted and one more constrained due to patriarchal ideology and traditional socio-cultural factors. Right time has come to women to get their due share in various developmental programmes. Empowerment is a process that aims to alter the existing systemic forces which marginalise and degrade women. One of the important goal of women empowerment is to challenge patriarchal ideology and this will provide the solution for many social evils such as violence against women, high population growth rates, environmental degradation, illiteracy, ill-health, unemployment and in general low status of women. The process of development would be incomplete, unless women are fully involved in it.

Advancing gender equality and equity, the empowerment of women, elimination of all kinds of violence against women, ensuring the women's abilty to control their own fertility are the cornerstones of the population and development-related programme. The declaration and programme of action of the World Summit for Social Development—Copenhegan, 1995 called for equal educational and work opportunities for women.

The most innovative strategy which is today emerging as a unique response to the challenge of equality, development and peace is empowerment of women. The new perception implies that if the women are empowered, then there is stability in the society, achievement in all corners of the development including education, health care, eradication of poverty and slow population growth. If women are to be empowered, it is necessary to provide our expanding networking of support services so that they are freed from their gender-related shackles (Dash, 2005). Education is the most important agent in the process of empowerment of women. Education is the strategic instrument has its impact on social and economic status of women. Apart from providing facilities for education of women, it is also important to train the women so as to enhance their skill, thinking ability self-confidence and participation in decision-making processes.

The Emancipation of women is an essential pre-requisite for economic development and social progress of the nation. Women must be recognised as a power in the development process. One of the most conspicuous feature of the term empowerment is that it contains the word power, which to sidestep philosophical debate, may be broadly defined as control over material assets, intellectual resources and ideology. The material assets over which control can be exercised may be physical, human, or financial such as land, water, forests, people's bodies and labour, money and access to money. Intellectual resources include knowledge, information and ideas. Control over ideology signifies the ability to generate, propagate, sustain and institutionalise specific sets of beliefs, attitudes. Values and behaviour—virtually determining how people perceive and function within given socio-economic and political environments. Power thus accrues to those control or are able to influence the distribution of material resources, knowledge, and the ideology that governs social relations in both public and private life. (Usha Sharma, 2001) The holistic development of the nation is possible only by utilising the resources of women population. Empowerment is the most important essential component for utilising women resources. Women empowerment cannot be ignored while framing various polices and programmes for socio-economic development.

Empowerment in its simplest form means the manifestation of redistribution of power that challenges patriarchal ideology and male dominance (Chandra, 1997). It is both a process and the result of the process. It is a process that enables women to gain access to and control of materials as well as information resources. The most significant feature of the term empowerment is that it contains the word power and it may be defined as control over material assets, intellectual resources and ideology. Intellectual resources would sharpen women's awareness and make them aware of their potential and this would go a long way in the empowerment of women and creating a gender just society. The process of challenging existing power relations, and of gaining greater control over the sources of power may be termed as empowerment (Batliwala, 1997). Empowerment helps women to access to the new world of knowledge and can be begin to make new information choices in both their personnel and public lives. Women empowerment process must evolve a new understanding of power and experiment with ways of democratising and sharing power building, new mechanisms for collective responsibility, decision-making and accountability.

NEED FOR WOMEN EMPOWERMENT

Women empowerment is a most vital component for sustainable development. Empowerment equips women to be socially knowledgeable, economically independent, personally self-reliant and politically participatory. It is a process that involves intellectual enlightenment, economical enrichment and social-emancipation on the part of women.

- Empowerment enables women to realise their full capacity and powers in all spheres of life.
- Empowerment creates enabling environment for equal access to greater participation and control over the means.
- The empowerment of women covers both an individual and collective transformation.
- Building up self-esteem and self-confidence and enhancing self-respect.
- Making socially aware of rights and economically independent and self-reliant.
- Better, smooth and improved quality of life.
- Empowerment is the key solution to many social evils.
- Empowerment is the best safeguard mechanism for violence against women.

SHG act as the agents of empowering the women. Empowerment is a long-term process of social transformation, which changes the expiring particular system and strengthen the farm of marginalized women and have no social awareness, economic independence and security. Thus SHG serves as a mean to empower rural marginalized women.

The empowerment theme runs strongly through all the third-world countries specially in the context of women. Most of the modern democracies and developing nations have a public agenda for the process of empowerment of women. The concept of women empowerment is the outcome of several important critiques and debates generated by women's movement and recommended by the series of world women's conferences held in the last two decades with United Nation's support.

The empowerment concept figured prominently as an objective in the World Summit for social development held in Copenhegen in March 1995. The Draft Declaration of the Third preparative committee adopted by the heads of the states and governments asserted the following:

> "We affirm that in both economic and social terms the most productive policies and investments are those which empower people to maximize their capacities, resources and opportunities."
>
> "Recognize that empowering people, particularly women, to strengthen their capacities is a main objective of development and its principle resource. Empowerment requires the full participation of people in the formulation, implementation and evaluation of decisions determining the functioning and the well-being of our societies". (World Summit for Social Development, 1995)

Empowerment is a process and is not, therefore something that can be given to people. The process of empowerment is both individual, and collective, since it is through involvement in groups that people most often begin to develop their awareness and the ability to organize to take action and bring about change.

At a workshop of Pacific women entitled 'Women, Development and Empowerment', Vanessa Griffen spoke about what empowerment means to her: To me, the word simply means: adding to women's power… to me, power means:

- having control, or gaining further control;
- having a say and being listened to;
- being able to define and create from a women's perspective;
- being able to influence social choices and decisions affecting the whole society (not just areas of society accepted as women's place); and
- being recognized and respected as equal citizens and human beings with a contribution to make.

Power means being able to make a contribution at all levels of society and not just in the home. Power also means have women's contribution recognized and valued (Vanessa Griffen, 1987).

Gender equality and empowerment of women has been recognized as a crucial component in activity development. The United Nations has developed eight important target indicators for global development in 2000 which was edited as millennium development targets:

- Eradication of poverty;
- Basic education for all;
- Gender equality;
- Women empowerment;
- Reducing infant mortality rate;
- Against the diseases of AIDS and Malaria;
- Environment protection; and
- International networking.

The Draft Country Paper—India for the 4th World Conference on Women, Beijing, 1995 proposed the qualitative and quantitative indicators for evaluating the women's empowerment (Sahay, 1998).

Qualitative Indicators of Empowerment

- Increase in self-esteem, individual and collective confidence.
- Increase in articulation, knowledge and awareness levels on issues affecting the community at large, and women in particular such as women's health, nutrition, reproductive rights, legal rights, literacy, etc., depending on the programme.
- Increase or decrease in personal leisure time and time for child care.
- Increase or decrease in work loads of women as result of the new programme.
- Changes in the roles and responsibilities in the family and in the community.
- Visible increase or decrease in levels of domestic violence and other forms of violence perpetrated on the women and girl child.
- Responses to, and changes, in social and other customs that are anti-women, e.g. child marriage, dowry, discrimination against widows, etc.

- Visible changes in women's participation levels, e.g. are more women attending public meetings, training programmes; are women demanding participation in other events related to their lives?
- Increase in bargaining/negotiating power of the women as an individual in the home and community as well as in collectives or women.
- Increased access to and ability to gather information and knowledge not only about the project, but about what affects their lives.
- Formation of cohesive and articulate women's groups/ collectives at the village level, district, block, state levels.
- Positive changes in social attitudes amongst the community member towards discrimination against women and the girl child.
- Awareness and recognition of women's economic contribution within and outside the household.
- Women's decision-making over the kind of work she is doing; is income and expenditure in her control or is she still subservient to member's in the family.

Quantitative Indicators of Empowerment

(a) Demographic Trends
  - maternal/mortality rates
  - fertility rates
  - sex ratio
  - life expectancy at birth
  - average age of marriage

(b) Number of women participating in different development programmes.

(c) Greater access and control over community resources/ government schemes/services, e.g. crèches, credit savings groups cooperatives, NFE centres, schools wells, etc.

(d) Visible changes in physical health status/nutritional levels.

(e) Changes in male/female literacy levels—primary, secondary and adult literacy including enrolment and retention rates.

(f) Participation levels of women in political processes at the local level.

FRAMEWORK FOR EMPOWERMENT

At present women development has become the prime concern of all countries. Women's development can be viewed in terms of five levels of equality, of which empowerment in an essential element at each level. The levels, according to Longwe (1990) are welfare, access, conscientization, participation and control.

1. WELFARE—the first level, addresses only the basic needs of women. without recognizing or attempting to solve the underlying structural causes, which necessitate provision of welfare services. At this point, women are merely passive beneficiaries of welfare benefits.

2. ACCESS—the second level is essential for women to make meaningful progress. The involves equality of access to resources, such as education opportunities, land and credit. The path of empowerment is initiated when women recognize their lack of access to resources as a barrier to their growth and overall well-being, and take action to address this.

3. CONSCIENTIZATION—is a crucial point in the Empowerment Framework. For women to take appropriate action to dose gender gaps or gender inequalities, there must be recognition that their problems stem form inherent structural and institutional discrimination. They must also recognize the role they can often play in reinforcing the system that restricts their growth

4. PARTICIPATION—is the point where women arc taking decisions alongside men equally. To reach this level, however, mobilization is necessary. By organising themselves and working collectively, women will be empowered aim increased representation, which will lead to increased empowerment and ultimately greater control.

5. CONTROL—is the ultimate level of equality and empowerment. Here the balance of power between men and women is, equal, and neither party has dominance over the other. At this stage in the Empowerment Framework, women are able to make decisions over their lives, and the lives of their children, and play an active role in the development process. Further, the contributions of women are fully recognized and rewarded.

Using the Empowerment Framework, development planners; can determine whether a project or programme is at the welfare, access, concretization, participation of control level, and determine the point of intervention, to move women to higher levels of equality and empowerment. An empowerment approach to development can also mean people's participation in the policy-making and planning processes.

COMPONENTS OF EMPOWERMENT

The subordinate position of women has many manifestations in the society. The limited representation of women in the formal political system, the presence of large number of women in the informal sector with reduced financial rewards, the near exclusive responsibilities for family and children, low level of aspiration and low self-esteem are some of the important manifestations of women's subordinate position.

The subordination of women has many facets so also the empowerment of women. Empowerment is a socio-political concept and goes beyond the formal political participation and awareness among women. A complete definition of empowerment includes the following components (Nelly P. Stromquist, *Encyclopedia of Women*, 1998). They are:

1. Cognitive component;
2. Psychological component;
3. Political component; and
4. Economic component.

The **cognitive component** refers to women's understanding of their conditions of subordination and the causes of condition at both micro and macro levels of society. It involves understanding the social and cultural process that structured gender relations and initiate actions to restructure the gender relationship. An important element of the cognitive component of empowerment is awareness about legal rights for women. This is important because in many democratically advanced nations the legislation for gender equity and women's rights are well ahead of practice. Therefore, women need to know the existing legal rights in order to improve their social position. The cognitive component also involves the need to understand the conjugal rights and duties for women.

The **psychological component** include the developments of positive feelings among women so that they can confidently initiate the actions against all forms of oppression.

The **political component** includes the ability of women to analyses socio-political environment and the ability to organize and mobilize themselves for social change. Therefore, the empowerment process involves political awareness and collective action by women for social transformation.

The **economic component** involves participation of women in income generation activities and releasing economic independence. This is very important since it complements the development of other components of empowerment.

The important step of empowerment process is the women to come out from household activities and participate in community management roans in the form of elective understand, this will develop a sense of independence of the competence and solidarity our women. In the creation of small cohesive group will make women to learn the leadership qualities and other competence. The members in the group will develop in sense of self-esteem, self-confidence, competence, braveness and attorney.

POLICY APPROACHES TO THIRD WORLD WOMEN

Welfare Approach—Introduced in the year 1950s and 1960s, welfare is the earliest policy approach concerned with women in developing countries. Its purpose is to bring women into development as better mothers. Women are seen as passive beneficiaries of development. The reproductive role of women is recognised and policy seeks to meet practical gender needs through that role by top-down handouts of food aid, measures against malnutrition and family planning. It is non-challenging and therefore still widely popular.

Equity Approach—Equity is the original 'WID' approach, introduced within the 1975-85 UN women's Decade. Its purpose is to gain equity for women in the development process. Women are seen as active participants in development. It recognises women's triple role and seeks to meet strategic gender needs through direct state intervention, giving political and economic autonomy to women, and reducing inequality with men. It challenges women's subordinate position.

Anti-Poverty Approach—It is the second WID approach, the "toned down" version of equity, introduced from 1970s onwards. Its purpose is to ensure that poor women increase their productivity. Women's poverty is seen as the problem of underdevelopment, not of subordination. It recognises the productive role of women and seeks to meet practical gender needs to earn an income particularly through small scale income generating projects

Efficiency Approach—Efficiency is the third and now predominant WID approach, particularly since the 1980s debit crisis. Its purpose is to ensure that development is more efficient and effective through women's economic contribution. Women's participation is equated with equity for women. It seeks to meet practical gender needs while relying on all of women's three roles and an elastic concept of women's time. Women are seen primarily in terms of their capacity to compensate for declining social services by extending their working day.

Empowerment Approach—Empowerment is the most recent approach that tried to integrate women into pre-existing structures, raising questions about the causes of women's subordination and advocating bottom up women's organizations as the focal point for achieving a participatory women's development. Its purpose is to empower women through greater self-reliance. Women's subordination is seen not only as the problem of men but also of colonial and neo-colonial oppression. It recognises women's triple role, and seeks to meet strategic gender needs indirectly through bottom-up mobilization around practical gender needs. It is potentially challenging, although it avoids the criticism of being western-inspired feminism.

The governmental agencies have adopted the concept of empowerment and established programmers such as the national literacy mission, women's development and the Panchayatraj schemes, aimed at 'empowering' people, especially women. The Indian government's country paper for the summit includes of section "Empowering the people models of mobilization." This takes along empowering the poor to enable them to help themselves and removing social, economic, cultural and psychological barriers to transform them from 'pamire recipients' of government programmes to active participants and managers of their own affairs, there is a notion of empowerment which involve organizing them into informed groups, formal trade unions, co-operatives, etc. for exciting collective pressure, articulating demand and effectively participating in the decision-making process with the ultimate objective of building foundations of individuals and collective self-reliance (Government of India, 1995).

In recent years in the context of shifting development of the state on the one hand, and the resurgence of people's movement on the other the issues of the social development and empowerment of marginalized groups have acquired significance among policy planners, social activities and academic of diverse intellectual pursuits. Over the last five decades, the thrust of development has been shifted in India from one sector to another, and also from one direction to another. Accordingly, the priorities in the area of action for different target groups and consequent strategies have also been reformulated to suit the changing perceptions. Immediately after independence, development strategy in India was concerned with the issue of 'growth with stability'. The concept of overall development of society of the fifties, known as community development, which aimed at the development of the entire population, was shifted in the mid-sixties to understand development, specifically of the poor. Thus, from the early concern for 'growth with social entice'. Significantly, in the context of globalization and the new economic order in the eighties and nineties, the notion of 'development with empowerment' got a new coinage re-orienting the pre-existing social development towards a process of sharing of power. (Debal K. Singha Roy, 2001)

NATIONAL POLICY FOR THE EMPOWERMENT OF WOMEN, 2001

The Government of India have adopted the concept of empowerment and established programmes such as the National Literacy mission, Women's development and the panchayatiraj schemes aimed at empowering people, especially women. The Indian government's country paper for the Copenhegen Summit includes a section "Empowering the people a models of mobilization. This talks about empowering the poor to enable them to help themselves and removing social, economic, cultural and psychological barriers to transform them from "Passive recipients" of government programmes to active participants and managers of their own affairs". Here is a notion of empowerment which involves organising them into informal groups, formal associations, trade unions, cooperatives, etc. for exerting collective pressure articulating demand and effectively participating in the decision-making process with the ultimate objective of building foundations of individual and collective self-reliance (GOI, 1995).

Indian constitution enshrined the principle of gender equality in its preamble, fundamental rights, fundamental duties and directive principles. The constitution also empowers the state to adopt measures of positive dissemination in favour of women.

Our Indian democratic polity, legal provisions, development policies, plans and programmes have aimed at women's advancement in different spheres. From the Fifth Five Year Plan (1974-78) onwards, there has been a marker shift in the approach to women's issues from welfare to development. In recent years, the empowerment of women has been recognized as the central issue in determining the status of women. The National Commission for Women was set-up by an Act of Parliament in 1990 to safeguard the rights and legal entitlements of women. The 73rd and 74th Amendments (1993) to the Constitution of India have provided for reservation of seats in the local bodies of Panchayats and Municipalities for women, laying a strong foundation for their participation in decision-making at the local levels. India has also ratified various international conventions and human rights instruments committing to secure equal rights of women. Key among them is the ratification of the Convention on Elimination of All Forms of Discrimination Against Women (CEDAW) in 1993. The Mexico Plan of Action (1975), the Nairobi Forward Looking Strategies (1985), the Beijing Declaration as well as the Platform for Action (1995) and the Outcome Document adopted by the UNGA Session on Gender Equality and Development & Peace for the 21st century, titled "Further actions and initiatives to implement the Beijing Declaration and the Platform for Action" have been unreservedly endorsed by India for appropriate follow-up.

The Policy also takes note of the commitments of the Ninth Five Year Plan and the other Sectoral Policies relating to Empowerment of Women. The women's movement and a wide-spread network of non-Government Organisations which have strong grassroots presence and deep insight into women's concerns have contributed in inspiring initiatives for the empowerment of women. However, there still exists a wide gap between the goals enunciated in the Constitution, legislation, policies, plans, programmes, and related mechanisms on the one hand and the situational reality of the status of women in India, on the other. This has been analyzed extensively in the Report of the Committee on the Status of Women in India, "Towards Equality", 1974 and highlighted in the National Perspective Plan for Women, 1988-2000, the Shramshakti Report, 1988 and the "Platform for Action, Five Years After—An Assessment". Gender disparity manifests itself in various forms, the most obvious being the trend of continuously declining female ratio in the population in the last few decades. Social stereotyping and violence at the domestic and societal levels are some of the other manifestations. Discrimination against girl children, adolescent girls and women persists in parts of the country.

The underlying causes of gender inequality are related to social and economic structure, which is based on informal and formal norms and practices. Consequently, the access of women particularly those belonging to weaker sections including Scheduled Castes/ Scheduled Tribes/Other Backward Classes and minorities, majority of whom are in the rural areas and in the informal, unorganized sector—to education, health and productive resources, among others, is inadequate. Therefore, they remain largely marginalized, poor and socially excluded.

The goal of this Policy is to bring about the advancement, development and empowerment of women. The Policy will be widely disseminated so as to encourage active participation of all stakeholders for achieving its goals. Specifically, the objectives of this Policy include:

(i) Creating an environment through positive economic and social policies for full development of women to enable them to realize their full potential;

(ii) The *de-jure* and *de-facto* enjoyment of all human rights and fundamental freedom by women on equal basis with men in all spheres—political, economic, social, cultural and civil;

(iii) Equal access to participation and decision-making of women in social, political and economic life of the nation;

(iv) Equal access to women to health care, quality education at all levels, career and vocational guidance, employment, equal remuneration, occupational health and safety, social security and public office, etc.;

(v) Strengthening legal systems aimed at elimination of all forms of discrimination against women;

(vi) Changing societal attitudes and community practices by active participation and involvement of both men and women;

(vii) Mainstreaming a gender perspective in the development process;

(viii) Elimination of discrimination and all forms of violence against women and the girl child; and

(ix) Building and strengthening partnerships with civil society, particularly women's organizations.

Policy Prescriptions

Judicial Legal Systems

Legal-judicial system will be make more responsive and gender sensitive to women's needs, especially in cases of domestic violence and personal assault. New laws will be enacted and existing laws reviewed to ensure that justice is quick and the punishment meted out to the culprits is commensurate with the severity of the offence.

At the initiative of and with the full participation of all stakeholders including community and religious leaders, the Policy would aim to encourage changes in personal laws such as those related to marriage, divorce, maintenance and guardianship so as to eliminate discrimination against women.

The evolution of property rights in a patriarchal system has contributed to the subordinate status of women. The Policy would aim to encourage changes in laws relating to ownership of property and inheritance by evolving consensus in order to make them gender just.

Decision-making

Women's equality in power sharing and active participation in decision-making, including decision-making in political process at all levels will be ensured for the achievement of the goals of empowerment. All measures will be taken to guarantee women equal access to and full participation in decision-making bodies at every level, including the legislative, executive, judicial, corporate, statutory bodies, as also the advisory Commissions, Committees, Boards, Trusts, etc. Affirmative action such as reservations/quotas, including in higher legislative bodies, will be considered whenever necessary on a time-bound basis. Women-friendly personnel policies will also be drawn up to encourage women to participate effectively in the developmental process.

Mainstreaming a Gender Perspective in the Development Process

Policies, programmes and systems will be established to ensure mainstreaming of women's perspectives in all developmental processes, as catalysts, participants and recipients. Wherever there are gaps in policies and programmes, women specific interventions would be undertaken to bridge these. Coordinating and monitoring mechanisms will also be devised to assess from time to time the progress of such mainstreaming mechanisms. Women's issues and concerns as a result will specially be addressed and reflected in all concerned laws, sectoral policies, plans and programmes of action.

Economic Empowerment of Women

Poverty Eradication

Since women comprise the majority of the population below the poverty line and are very often in situations of extreme poverty, given the harsh realities of intra-household and social discrimination, macro-economic policies and poverty eradication programmes will specifically address the needs and problems of such women. There will be improved implementation of programmes which are already women-oriented with special targets for women. Steps will be taken for mobilization of poor women and convergence of services, by offering them a range of economic and social options, along with necessary support measures to enhance their capabilities.

Micro-Credit

In order to enhance women's access to credit for consumption and production, the establishment of new, and strengthening of existing micro-credit mechanisms and micro-finance institutions will be undertaken so that the outreach of credit is enhanced. Other supportive measures would be taken to ensure adequate flow of credit through extant financial institutions and banks, so that all women below poverty line have easy access to credit.

Women and Economy

Women's perspectives will be included in designing and implementing macro-economic and social policies by institutionalizing their participation in such processes. Their contribution to socio-economic development as producers and workers will be recognized in the formal and informal sectors (including home-based workers) and appropriate policies relating to employment and to her working conditions will be drawn up. Such measures could include:

(a) Reinterpretation and redefinition of conventional concepts of work wherever necessary, e.g. in the Census records, to reflect women's contribution as producers and workers.
(b) Preparation of satellite and national accounts.
(c) Development of appropriate methodologies for undertaking (i) and (ii) above.

Globalization

Globalization has presented new challenges for the realization of the goal of women's equality, the gender impact of which has not been systematically evaluated fully. However, from the micro-level studies that were commissioned by the Department of Women & Child Development, it is evident that there is a need for re-framing policies for access to employment and quality of employment. Benefits of the growing global economy have been unevenly distributed leading to wider economic disparities, the feminization of poverty, increased gender inequality through often deteriorating working conditions and unsafe working environment especially in the informal economy and rural areas. Strategies will be designed to enhance the capacity of women and empower them to meet the negative social and economic impacts, which may flow from the globalization process.

Women and Agriculture

In view of the critical role of women in the agriculture and allied sectors, as producers, concentrated efforts will be made to ensure that benefits of training, extension and various programmes will reach them in proportion to their numbers. The programmes for training women in soil conservation, social forestry, dairy development and other occupations allied to agriculture like horticulture, livestock including small animal husbandry, poultry, fisheries, etc. will be expanded to benefit women workers in the agriculture sector.

Women and Industry

The important role-played by women in electronics, information technology and food processing and agro-industry and textiles has been crucial to the development of these sectors. They would be given comprehensive support in terms of labour legislation, social security and other support services to participate in various industrial sectors.

Women at present cannot work in night shift in factories even if they wish to. Suitable measures will be taken to enable women to work in night shift in factories. This will be accompanied with support services for security, transportation, etc.

Support Services

The provision of support services for women, like child care facilities, including crèches at work places and educational institutions, homes for the aged and the disabled will be expanded and improved to create an enabling environment and to ensure their full cooperation in social, political and economic life. Women-friendly personnel policies will also be drawn up to encourage women to participate effectively in the developmental process.

Social Empowerment of Women

Education

Equal access to education for women and girls will be ensured. Special measures will be taken to eliminate discrimination, universalize education, eradicate illiteracy, create a gender-sensitive educational system, increase enrolment and retention rates of girls and improve the quality of education to facilitate life-long learning as well as development of vocational/technical skills by women. Reducing the gender gap in secondary and higher education would be a focus area. Sectoral time targets in existing policies will be achieved, with a special focus on girls and women, particularly those belonging to weaker sections including the Scheduled Castes/ Scheduled Tribes/Other Backward Classes/Minorities. Gender sensitive curricula would be developed at all levels of educational system in order to address sex stereotyping as one of the causes of gender discrimination.

Health

A holistic approach to women's health which includes both nutrition and health services will be adopted and special attention will be given to the needs of women and the girls at all stages of the life cycle. The reduction of infant mortality and maternal mortality, which are sensitive indicators of human development, is a priority concern. This policy reiterates the national demographic goals for Infant Mortality Rate (IMR), Maternal Mortality Rate (MMR) that are set out in the National Population Policy, 2000. Women should have access to comprehensive, affordable and quality health care. Measures will be adopted that take into account the reproductive rights of women to enable them to exercise informed choices, their vulnerability to sexual and health problems together with endemic, infectious and communicable diseases such as malaria, TB, and water borne diseases as well as hypertension and cardio-pulmonary diseases. The social, developmental and health consequences of HIV/AIDS and other sexually transmitted diseases will be tackled from a gender perspective.

To effectively meet problems of infant and maternal morality, and early marriage, the availability of good and accurate data at micro-level on deaths, birth and marriages is required. Strict implementation of registration of births and deaths would be ensured and registration of marriages would be made compulsory.

In accordance with the commitment of the National Population Policy (2000) to population stabilization, this Policy recognizes the critical need of men and women to have access to safe, effective and affordable methods of family planning of their choice and the need to suitably address the issues of early marriages and spacing of children. Interventions such as spread of education, compulsory registration of marriage and special programmes like Balika Samridhi Yojana should impact on delaying the age of marriage so that by 2010 child marriages are eliminated.

Women's traditional knowledge about health care and nutrition will be recognized through proper documentation and its use will be encouraged. The use of Indian and alternative systems of medicine will be enhanced within the framework of overall health infrastructure available for women.

Nutrition

In view of the high risk of malnutrition and disease that women face at all the three critical stages viz., infancy and childhood, adolescent and reproductive phase, focused attention would be paid to meeting the nutritional needs of women at all stages of the life cycle. This is also important in view of the critical link between the health of adolescent girls, pregnant and lactating women with the health of infant and young children. Special efforts will be made to tackle the problem of macro and micro-nutrient deficiencies especially amongst pregnant and lactating women as it leads to various diseases and disabilities.

Intra-household discrimination in nutritional matters *vis-à-vis* girls and women will be sought to be ended through appropriate strategies. Widespread use of nutrition education would be made to address the issues of intra-household imbalances in nutrition and the special needs of pregnant and lactating women. Women's participation will also be ensured in the planning, superintendence and delivery of the system.

Drinking Water and Sanitation

Special attention will be given to the needs of women in the provision of safe drinking water, sewage disposal, toilet facilities and sanitation within accessible reach of households, especially in rural areas and urban slums. Women's participation will be ensured in the planning, delivery and maintenance of such services.

Housing and Shelter

Women's perspectives will be included in housing policies, planning of housing colonies and provision of shelter both in rural and urban areas. Special attention will be given for providing adequate and safe housing and accommodation for women including single woman, heads of households, working women, students, apprentices and trainees.

Environment

Women will be involved and their perspectives reflected in the policies and programmes for environment, conservation and restoration. Considering the impact of environmental factors on their livelihoods, women's participation will be ensured in the conservation of the environment and control of environmental degradation. The vast majority of rural women still depend on the locally available non-commercial sources of energy such as animal dung, crop waste and fuel wood. In order to ensure the efficient use of these energy resources in an environmental-friendly manner, the Policy will aim at promoting the programmes of non-conventional energy resources. Women will be involved in spreading the use of solar energy, biogas, smokeless chulhas and other rural application so as to have a visible impact of these measures in influencing eco-system and in changing the life styles of rural women.

Science and Technology

Programmes will be strengthened to bring about a greater involvement of women in science and technology. These will include measures to motivate girls to take up science and technology for higher education and also ensure that development projects with scientific and technical inputs involve women fully. Efforts to develop a scientific temper and awareness will also be stepped up. Special measures would be taken for their training in areas where they have special skills like communication and information technology. Efforts to develop appropriate technologies suited to women's needs as well as to reduce their drudgery will be given a special focus too.

Women in Difficult Circumstances

In recognition of the diversity of women's situations and in acknowledgement of the needs of specially disadvantaged groups, measures and programmes will be undertaken to provide them with special assistance. These groups include women in extreme poverty, destitute women, women in conflict situations, women affected by natural calamities, women in less developed regions, the disabled widows, elderly women, single women in difficult circumstances, women heading households, those displaced from employment, migrants, women who are victims of marital violence, deserted women and prostitutes, etc.

Violence Against Women

All forms of violence against women, physical and mental, whether at domestic or societal levels, including those arising from customs, traditions or accepted practices shall be dealt with effectively with a view to eliminate its incidence. Institutions and mechanisms/ schemes for assistance will be created and strengthened for prevention of such violence, including sexual harassment at work place and customs like dowry; for the rehabilitation of the victims of violence and for taking effective action against the perpetrators of such violence. A special emphasis will also be laid on programmes and measures to deal with trafficking in women and girls.

Rights of the Girl Child

All forms of discrimination against the girl child and violation of her rights shall be eliminated by undertaking strong measures both preventive and punitive within and outside the family. These would relate specifically to strict enforcement of laws against prenatal sex selection and the practices of female foeticide, female infanticide, child marriage, child abuse and child prostitution, etc. Removal of discrimination in the treatment of the girl child will be actively fostered. There will be special emphasis on the needs of the girl child and earmarking of substantial investments in the areas relating to food and nutrition, health and education, and in vocational education. In implementing programmes for elimination child labour, there will be a special focus on girl children.

Mass Media

Media will be used to portray images consistent with human dignity of girls and women. The Policy will specifically strive to remove demeaning, degrading and negative conventional stereotypical images of women and violence against women. Private sector partners and media networks will be involved at all levels to ensure equal access for women particularly in the area of information and communication technologies. The media would be encouraged to develop codes of conduct, professional guidelines and other self-regulatory mechanisms to remove gender stereotypes and promote balanced portrayals of women and men.

Operational Strategies

Action Plans

All Central and State Ministries will draw up time-bound Action Plans for translating the Policy into a set of concrete actions, through a participatory process of consultation with Centre/State Departments of Women and Child Development and National/State Commissions for Women. The Plans will specifically including the following:

- Measurable goals to be achieved by 2010.
- Identification and commitment of resources.
- Responsibilities for implementation of action points.
- Structures and mechanisms to ensure efficient monitoring, review and gender impact assessment of action points and policies.
- Introduction of a gender perspective in the budgeting process.

In order to support better planning and programme formulation and adequate allocation of resources, Gender Development Indices (GDI) will be developed by networking with specialized agencies. These could be analyzed and studied in depth. Gender auditing and development of evaluation mechanisms will also be undertaken alongside.

Collection of gender disaggregated data by all primary data collecting agencies of the Central and State Governments as well as Research and Academic Institutions in the Public and Private Sectors will be undertaken. Data and information gaps invital areas reflecting the status of women will be sought to be filled in by these immediately. All Ministries/Corporations/Banks and financial institutions, etc. will be advised to collect, collate, disseminate and maintain/publish date related to programmes and benefits on a gender disaggregated basis. This will help in meaningful planning and evaluation of policies.

Institutional Mechanisms

Institutional mechanisms, to promote the advancement of women, which exist at the Central and State levels, will be strengthened. These will be through interventions as may be appropriate and will relate to among others, provision of adequate resources, training and advocacy skills to effectively influence macro-policies, legislation, programmes, etc. to achieve the empowerment of women.

National and State Councils will be formed to oversee the operationalisation of the Policy on a regular basis. The National Council will be headed by the Prime Minister and the State Councils by the Chief Ministers and will be broad in composition having representatives from the concerned Department/Ministries, National and State Commissions for Women, Social Welfare Board, representatives of Non-Government Organizations, Women's Organizations, Corporate Sector, Trade Unions, financing institutions, academics, experts and social activists, etc. These bodies will review the progress made in implementing the Policy twice a year. The National Development Council will also be informed of the progress of the programme undertaken under the policy from time to time for advice and comments.

National and State Resource Centres on women will be established with mandate for collection and dissemination of information, undertaking research work, conducting surveys, implementing training and awareness generation programmes, etc. These Centres will link up with Women's Studies Centres and other research and academic institutions through suitable information networking systems.

While institutions at the district level will be strengthened, at the grassroots, women will be helped by Government through its programmes to organize and strengthen into Self-Help Groups (SHG) at the Anganwadi/Village/Town level. The women's groups will be helped to institutionalize themselves into registered societies and to federate at the Panchayat/Municipal level. These societies will bring about synergistic implementation of all the social and economic development programmes by drawing resources made available through Government and Non-Government channels, including banks and financial institutions and by establishing a close interface with the Panchayats/Municipalities.

Resource Management

Availability of adequate financial, human and market resources to implement the Policy will be managed by concerned Departments, financial credit institutions and banks, private sector, civil society and other connected institutions. This process will include:

(a) Assessment of benefits flowing to women and resource allocation to the programmes relating to them through an exercise of gender budgeting. Appropriate changes in policies will be made to optimize benefits to women under these schemes;

(b) Adequate resource allocation to develop and promote the policy outlined earlier based on (a) above by concerned Departments;

(c) Developing synergy between personnel of Health, Rural Development, Education and Women & Child Development Department at field level and other village level functionaries; and

(d) Meeting credit needs by banks and financial credit institutions through suitable policy initiatives and development of new institutions in coordination with the Department of Women & Child Development.

The Strategy of Women's Component Plan adopted in the Ninth Plan of ensuring that not less than 30% of benefits/funds flow to women from all Ministries and Departments will be implemented effectively so that the needs and interests of women and girls are addressed by all concerned sectors. The Department of Women and Child Development being the nodal Ministry will monitor and review the progress of the implementation of the Component Plan from time to time, in terms of both quality and quantity in collaboration with the Planning Commission.

Efforts will be made to channelize private sector investments too, to support programmes and projects for advancement of women.

Legislation

The existing legislative structure will be reviewed and additional legislative measures taken by identified departments to implement the Policy. This will also involve a review of all existing laws including personal, customary and tribal laws, subordinate legislation, related rules as well as executive and administrative regulations to eliminate all gender discriminatory references. The process will be planned over a time period 2000-03. The specific measures required would be evolved through a consultation process involving civil society, National Commission for Women and Department of Women and Child Development. In appropriate cases the consultation process would be widened to include other stakeholders too.

Effective implementation of legislation would be promoted by involving civil society and community. Appropriate changes in legislation will be undertaken, if necessary.

In addition, following other specific measures will be taken to implement the legislation effectively:

- Strict enforcement of all relevant legal provisions and speedy redressal of grievances will be ensured, with a special focus on violence and gender-related atrocities;
- Measures to prevent and punish sexual harassment at the place of work, protection for women workers in the organized/unorganized sector and strict enforcement of relevant laws such as Equal Remuneration Act and Minimum Wages Act will be undertaken;
- Crimes against women, their incidence, prevention, investigation, detection and prosecution will be regularly reviewed at all Crime Review fora and conferences at the Central, State and District levels. Recognised, local, voluntary organizations will be authorized to lodge complaints and facilitate registration, investigations and legal proceedings related to violence and atrocities against girls and women;
- Women's Cells in Police Stations, Women Police Stations, Family Courts, Mahila Courts, Counselling Centers, Legal Aid Centers and Nyaya Panchayats will be strengthened and

expanded to eliminate violence and atrocities against women; and

- Widespread dissemination of information on all aspects of legal rights, human rights and other entitlements of women, through specially designed legal literacy programmes and rights information programmes will be done.

Gender Sensitization

Training of personnel of executive, legislative and judicial wings of the State, with a special focus on policy and programme framers, implementation and development agencies, law enforcement machinery and the judiciary, as well as non-governmental organizations will be undertaken. Other measures will include:

- Promoting societal awareness to gender issues and women's human rights;
- Review of curriculum and educational materials to include gender education and human rights issues;
- Removal of all references derogatory to the dignity of women from all public documents and legal instruments; and
- Use of different forms of mass media to communicate social messages relating to women's equality and empowerment.

Panchayati Raj Institutions

The 73rd and 74th Amendments (1993) to the Indian Constitution have served as a breakthrough towards ensuring equal access and increased participation in political power structure for women. The PRIs will play a central role in the process of enhancing women's participation in public life. The PRIs and the local self-Governments will be actively involved in the implementation and execution of the National Policy for Women at the grassroots level.

Partnership with the Voluntary Sector Organizations

The involvement of voluntary organizations, associations, federations, trade unions, non-governmental organizations, women's organizations, as well as institutions dealing with education, training and research will be ensured in the formulation, implementation, monitoring and review of all policies and programmes affective women. Towards this end, they will be provided with appropriate support related to resources and capacity building and facilitated to participate actively in the process of the empowerment of women.

International Cooperation

The Policy will aim at implementation of international obligations/commitments in all sectors on empowerment of women such as the Convention on All Forms of Discrimination Against Women (CEDAW), Convention of the Rights of the Child (CRC), International Conference of Population and Development (ICPD+5) and other such instruments. International, regional and sub-regional cooperation towards the empowerment of women will continue to be encouraged through sharing of experiences, exchange of ideas and technology, networking with institutions and organizations and through bilateral and multi-lateral partnerships.

GREAT PERSONALITIES ABOUT WOMEN EMPOWERMENT

Mahatma Gandhi

Gandhi was a passionate lover of humanity and an implacable enemy of all injustice and inequality and friend of downtrodden. He had almost an instinctive understanding of women and their problems, and had a deep and abiding sympathy for them. He has stated that *"women are the noblest of God's creation, supreme in their own sphere of activity"*.

In a letter written to Rajkumari Amrit Kaur from Wardha in the year 1936 Gandhi writes, "If you women would only realise your dignity and privilege and make full use of it for mankind, you will make it much better than it is. But man has delighted in enslaving you and you have proved willing till the slaves and the slave holders have become one in the crime of degrading humanity. My special function from childhood, you might say, has been to make women realise her dignity. I was once slave-holder myself but Ba proved an unwilling slave and thus 'opened my eyes to my mission'." Gandhi said: I am uncompromising in the matter of woman's rights. In my opinion she should labour under no legal disability not suffered by man. I should treat daughters and sons on a footing of perfect equality. Again he said, "To call woman the weaker sex is a libel; it is man's injustice to woman. If by strength is meant moral power, then woman is immeasurably man's superior. Has she not great intuition, is she not more self-sacrificing, has she not great powers of endurance, has she not greater courage? Without her man could not be. If non-violence is the law of our being, the future is with woman. He described discrimination against woman as an anachronism as already stated." He said: "I fail to see any reason for jubilation over the birth of a son and for mourning over that of a daughter. Both are God's gifts. They have an equal right to live and are equally necessary to keep the world going."

Prof. K.D. Gangrade rightly said that the pursuit of power be not the only aim of empowerment. It should be their "total emancipation". No one can double the efforts made by Gandhi to empower women. He had attracted so many millions of not only literate but illiterate women without the power of the state, without the modern information technology and offering in return only sweat, toil and pain, is an exceptional feat!. His insistence on women's education is the first step in the right direction as—

Educating a man is
 Educating an individual
Educating a woman is
 Educating a society

We still have miles to go to achieve our cherished goal to empower women.

Jawaharlal Nehru, India's first Prime Minister

Nehru emphasised the need for a special policy towards women empowerment. He wrote: "we talk about a welfare state and direct our energies towards its realisation. That welfare must be the common property of everyone in India, and not the monopoly of the privileged groups as it is today. If I may be allowed to lay greater stress on some, they would be the welfare of children, the status of women and the welfare of the tribal and hilly people in our country. Women in India have a background of history and tradition behind them, which is inspiring. It is true, however, that they have suffered much from various kinds of suppression and all these have to go so that they can play their full part in the life of the nation".

"When women moves forward, the family moves, the village moves and the Nation moves."

Smt. Indira Gandhi

"Women's Liberation is not a luxury for India, but an urgent necessity to enable the Nation to move ahead to a life which is more than satisfying materially, intellectually and spiritually."

Dr. Radhakrishnan

Radhakrishnan had viewed that "the progress of our land cannot be achieved without active participation of our mothers, wives, sisters and daughters."

Nobel Laureate Dr. Amartya Sen

Sen sees development as freedom which in turn empowers. He emphasizes, "Indeed the empowerment of women is one of the central issues in the process of development for many countries in the world today."

Dr. C. Rangarajan, former Governor of RBI

Rangarajan has rightly pointed out that initiating and monitoring the credit programmes for the poor can be made more effective and less costly if banks make attempt to organize the poor in self-help group women to ensure proper utilisation of credit and prompt repayment of loans.

Impact of Women Empowerment

Empowerment of women would mean equipping women to be economically independent, self-reliant, have a positive self-esteem to enable them to face any difficult situation and they should be able to participate in developmental activities. The empowered women should be able to participate in the process of decision-making. Education will be the only factor which would play the most crucial role in empowering women. As said by Sarala Gopalan that the pre-requisites for the empowerment of women are literacy and education, awareness, skill development, good health, access to economic resources, capacity and opportunity for participation in decision-making within the family, community and institutions of governance. Self-confidence, Self-reliant, Economic independence, access to resources, decision-making, political awareness and aware of Human Rights are the outcome of the women empowerment.

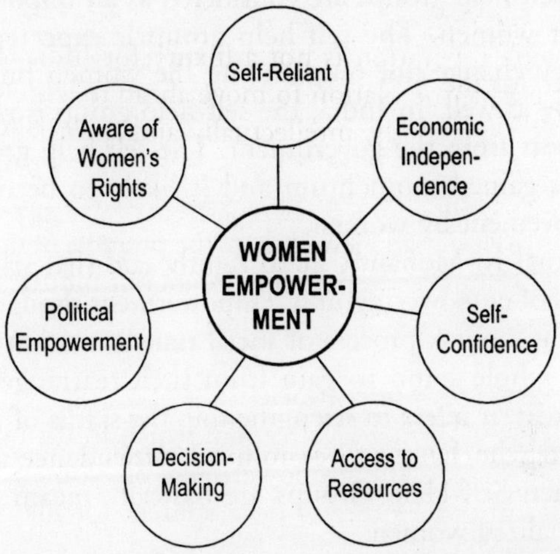

SELF-HELP GROUPS: AS A MOVEMENT

Empowerment is a process of awareness and capacity building, leading to greater participation, to greater decision-making power and control and transformative action. The empowerment of women covers both an individual and collective transformation. It strengthens their innate ability through acquiring knowledge, power and experience. Empowerment is a multifaceted process which encompasses many aspects enhancing awareness, increasing access to resource—economics, social and political, but of which an equally important component is the mobilisation and organisation of women into groups, because these groups form the basis for solidarity, strength and collective action. Organizations are accepted as an instrument to provide collective strength, greater bargaining power, articulate the voice of an interest group. They may also be recognised as a constituency to ensure representation of that section in local, national or international deliberate bodies/discussion fora (Debal, K., 2003)

There are a number of ways to empower women. However, organizing small and cohesive group of women with defined goals to attain is a fundamental requirement for any empowerment process. Realizing this the government along with non-governmental organizations started to organize small and cohesive group of women. These groups later came to be known as Women's Self-Help Groups.

Today, the self-help groups are considered as an important strategy to empower women. The self-help group is expected to bring a revolutionary change not only among the women but also in the wider society as well. In India, the self-help group is receiving very strong support from the government. The self-help group network in India has gained momentum and is likely to become a strong political movement by women.

Dr. Bimal K. Mohanty, 2006 rightly said that self-help group act as agents of empowering unit, empowerment though is normally understood as a quick process of social transformation whereby the people as a whole stand to gain from such rearrangement in the present context, it refers to strengthening the status of marginalized rural women who have no economic independence and security. Thus, Women Self-Help Groups are basically meant to empower rural marginalized women.

Self-help groups are proved to be very fruitful for empowerment of women. SHG promote saving habit, access to larger quantum of resources, group dynamics, leadership qualities, self-confidence, self-reliance, etc. In self-help groups collective action and solidarity is an important empowering mechanism. Collectivization implies cohesion of the group. Cohesion enables the members of the group to perceive common interests and act collectively. The emergence of SHG concept and its implementation is an innovative step for empower women mass in rural areas. It gives knowledge-based information and provides credit to rural women on easy terms with access to several income generating activities. The principle underlining the SHG modals in India include financing the poorest of the poor, ensuring excellent recovery level and empowering women not just by meeting their need for consumption and protective loans but also through more holistic educative programmes on issues such as sanitation, school enrolment and family planning, and Empowerment can be broadly categorised as social empowerment, economic empowerment and political empowerment. SHG approach is a key element for social, economic and political empowerment.

The empowerment of women through self-help groups would lead to benefits not only to the individual women and women groups but also for the family and community as a whole through collective action for development. These groups have a common perception of need and an impulse towards collective action. Empowering women is not just for meeting their economic needs but also through more holistic social development.

The concept of SHG serves to underline the principle "for the people, by the people, and of the people." The origin of SHG is from the brainchild of Gramin Bank of Bangladesh, which was founded by the Prof. Muhammad Yunus of Chittagong University in the year 1975. This was exclusively established for the poor. Self-help group is in small economically homogeneous and affinity group of rural poor which voluntarily agrees to contribute to a common fund to be lent to its members as per group decision, which works for group solidarity, self and group awareness, social and economic empowerment in the way of democratic functioning.

Characteristics of SHG

The important characteristics of self-help groups are small size, identical interest/social heritage/common occupation, homogeneity, affinity, intimate knowledge of members, intrinsic strength, needs and problems, flexible and responsive, democracy in operations, simple documentation, collective leadership, mutual discussions, group solidarity, self-help, awareness, social and economic empowerment.

Benefits

- A via media for development of savings habit among the poor,
- An access to larger quantum of resources,
- A window for better technology/skill upgradation,
- Availability of emergent, consumption/production credit Illustration the poor step,
- Access to various promotional assistance, and
- Assurance of freedom, quality, self-reliance and empowerment.

In self-help groups, collective action and solidarity is an important empowering mechanism. Collectivization implies cohesion of the group. Cohesion enables the members of the group to perceive common interests and act collectively.

Social Movement

Social movement is a prolonged action of deprived homogenous group to strengthen the roots of the group in the society to which the group belongs. The collective mobilization for action directed explicitly towards an alteration or transformation of the structure of a system, can be understood as a social movement. (P.N. Mukherji, 1977). Social movement which is an offshoot of social change may appear in any one of the stages of change depending upon certain system conditions. According to T.K. Oommen "...System characteristics of a society affect the ethos and style of social movement in that society which necessitate an analysis of three elements of society, namely the historicity, the elements of present social structure and the future vision of the society." Oommen defines, "Social movement as an institutionalized collective action, guided by an ideology and supported by an organisational structure". Mukherji analyses social movements as "A product of the social structure and the consequences for it, is and 'agent' of change, and at the same time it has a 'target' on which it operates". Social movement can be distinguished on the basis of the nature of change and ideology of the movement. "Movement can be aimed at reforms in one or another aspect of social life or oriented at bringing about changes in super ordinate or subordinate relationships and finally those oriented towards bringing about revolutionary change Illustration every sphere of life and in basic values". (Bhat, 1979).

Women's Movement

Throughout history women have collectively struggled against direct and indirect barriers to their self-development and their full social, political, and economic participation. The history of the women's movement is usually dated to the social reform movements of the nineteenth century and when campaigns for the betterment of the conditions of women's lives were taken up, initially by men. By the end of the century women had begun to organise themselves. Gradually they look up a number of causes such as education, conditions of women's work and so on. The women's organisations started struggle for women's rights in the early part of the twentieth century. At present, women movement focuses its attention on equality and empowerment. The activism within the women movement has influenced policy and planning of the government for development and empowerment.

Women's movements in general are directed by objectives, like to promote better understanding of the process of social, technological and environmental changes, to contribute to pursuit of human rights and to develop alternative concept, approach and strategies to bring out necessary changes for bettering the life of women with autonomy, freedom and full rights of the citizens. The women's movement and groups have to recognize the importance of the ways of empowering women.

Empowerment of Women as an Ideology

- Self-confidence building
- Increasing social awareness
- Functional literacy
- Awareness of legal rights and legal aid access
- Economic development—consisting of:
  - inculcating habit of savings
  - control over income and better management
  - change from worker status to work manager status

Collective Action

The collective organisation of SHG members and their activities, working pattern are analysed in the framework of a movement. For this study Self-Help Groups under Mahalir Thittam of Tamilnadu Women Development Corporation were undertaken.

The SHG is identified by a village level household survey, which provides the baseline the groups .are small in the range of 12-20 to facilitate sustainability. The age groups for the membership are 21 to 60. Preference is given for widows, divorcees, deserted and handicapped women and women belonging to SC/ST community. All members must be below the poverty line.

The group members meet every week for savings and repayment collections and every fortnight for discussing all other matters. The agenda is prepared and discussed in each meeting. The matters regarding savings, rotation of sangha funds, bank loans and repayments, social and community action programme are discussed in every meeting. Since the group functions in a democratic way one animator and two representatives are selected among the members instead of president, secretary and others. Animator will be the role model and a change agent for the village as a whole. The animator position will be rotated amongst the representatives once every two years.

Organizational Structure

The vision of Tamilnadu Women Development Corporation is "Empowerment of one million women in Tamilnadu with special emphasis on the poorest and disadvantaged, Social empowerment, economic empowerment and capacity building are the mission of the Mahalir Thittam. The self-help groups are supported by the above organisational structure.

Mahalir Thittam Mission Statement

- To build capacity of disadvantaged women in order that they are enabled to cross all social and economic barriers, and thereby facilitate their full development into empowered citizens.
- To achieve the equality of stages of women as participants, decision-makers and beneficiaries in the democratic, economic, social and cultural spheres of life.
- To create or reorient democratic, economic and social processes and institutions to enable women to participate fully and actively in decision-making in the family, community and at the local, district, state and national levels.
- To empower women to work together with men as equal partners and to inspire a new generation of women and men to work together for equality, sustainable development and communal harmony.
- To promote and ensure the human rights of women at all stages of their life cycle.

The Tamil Nadu Corporation for Development of Women Ltd. with its headquarters at Chennai is implementing the Muhalir Thittam project. The main objective is to combine the wide reach and resources available to the state, with the commitment and quality work of the NGOs. It has a project management unit. The unit consists of chairperson and managing director, executive director and general manager. Each district has a project implementation unit which is headed by a Project Officer, assisted by Assistant Project Officers in the various functional areas of training and communication, monitoring, schemes, marketing, administration and credit, co-ordination, monitoring the groups, conducting regular review meetings and organizing training programmes for NGOs and bankers are the role of the PlUs.

NGOs are another important unit that provide quality of work and commitment to this project at the grassroots level. They help to form groups and work continuously with the groups to make them strong, cohesive with and sustainable. They serve as adviser and facilitator to the groups on various matters such as social, economic and community action programmes. In order to understand the activity of the SHG in the framework of movement, some groups were selected and conducted a focus group interview with them. From the analysis it is found that the self-help groups are organised to manage their economic activities better and arc gaining empowerment in directions, which are appropriate to their needs, interests and constraints. They gained confidence from an increase in their relative financial independence and security. The increase in the literacy skills of the SHG members is another indicator of empowerment. Some of them learned to sign, to read and write and could do simple arithmetic work. The animators and representatives and SHG members got trained for this work by the NGOs with the help of Mahalir Thittam officials. The animators fell that through this one could develop certain leadership qualities such as organising meetings, liaison with NGOs and Government officials, coordinating and motivating the members.

Decision-making is the ultimate level of empowerment and equality. It signifies unit women have started taking control of their lives and situations through attending group meetings, public functions, involvement in income generating activities, joining other women in social causes. The collective and integrated activities of the SHG are presumed to have helped them in sustaining their family economically, giving better education to their children, meeting financial crises in the family, meeting any crisis independently. The SHG members are sensitized in acquiring an attitude of protest against various abuses, knowledge about their rights, and other social issues. Better communication skills is another indicator of empowerment. Most of the group members are attending the group meetings and Grama Sabha meeting regularly. This develops their ability to interact and communicate with each other. *Mutram* a monthly magazine projects the SHG activities of groups in Tamilnadu, creates a journalistic medium for the interaction of women at the grass-root level, and briefly explains the various schemes. Through this collective action with the ideology of empowerment Self-Help Groups are emerging as a movement in Tamilnadu.

SOCIAL IMPACT AND EMPOWERMENT OF WOMEN

TNCDW had initiated the Tamil Nadu Women's Development Project (TNWDP) assisted by IFAD during 1989-90. Its implementation and evaluation have thus, been considered as a landmark launch to open up a new global culture in gender equity. IFAD committed its funding to the tune of 13.15 million SDR for TNWDP for seven years with effect from 1989. The goal of TNWDP, as per appraisal report, is to establish a viable and replicable model for women's development, which could be adopted by agencies in other states.

The TNWDP aims at economic and social empowerment of rural poor women. This aim is sought to be attained through:

- institution building at the grassroots level through formation of women's Self-Help Groups and awareness creation through training and exposing the members to group dynamics;
- organizing the rural poor women to mobilize savings and to expose the members to group loaning and repayment ethics;
- providing access to credit for pursuing income generating activities to enhance income of the beneficiaries to raise them above the poverty levels; and
- ensuring group sustainability to achieve the goal of economic and social empowerment.

The TNWDP was designed to promote, through improvement in the social and economic status of rural women, empowerment of women in the 18-55 age group, particularly those families living below the poverty line defined as having an annual income of

Rs. 6400 and whose families have not been the recipient of any benefits under any other government programme. Within this overall target group with incomes less than Rs. 6400 per year, preference was to be given to families with an annual income below Rs. 3500. The target group also included landless women and women from small and marginal farm households and female headed households.

The project, implemented since 1989-90 initially in Dharmapuri district and subsequently in Salem and South Arcot districts during 1991-92, was further extended to Madurai and Ramanathapuram in 1993-94 covering in all 5 districts.

The IFAD project's primary concern was the holistic growth of poorest rural women to attain empowerment through a bi-focal approach of social and economic development. The focus of the economic impact was to facilitate the group members to cross the hurdle of poverty threshold. Following paragraphs sum up the achievements and shortcomings in this respect.

Achievements

About 64.24 percent of the beneficiary families under IFAD Project had crossed the poverty line. Two out of three families succeeded in crossing the poverty level. Nearly two-thirds or two out of three families had enjoyed an income level exceeding Rs. 11,000. Though the activities were no of high profile but only low-tech and low-risk alternatives, the beneficiary families were making a healthy transition from their disadvantaged contextual situation to a take-off stage as a result of IFAD assistance. Beneficiaries in the income bracket of Rs. 6401-11,000 during the pre-project did remarkably well. Family income range of Rs. 6400-11,000 provided the needed motivation and thrust for BPL families to aspire to graduate into the lower middle class status. Just 0.6 percent was in the income bracket of less than Rs. 3500. Two-thirds of the beneficiaries shared up to 64.13 percent of the total family income. IGP income to total family income was almost two-thirds indicating the potential of IGP activities.

The per capita income of the beneficiaries was trebled in the income group of <Rs. 3500; was doubled in the income category of Rs. 3501-4800; in all other high income brackets this had risen by 95-116 percent.

Horticultural activities took the lead with an annual average growth rate of 25.68 percent followed by goatery with 18.63 percent, milch animal with coconut grooves accounting for 15.71, milk business with 16.81 percent and milch animals 12.37 percent.

80 percent of the beneficiaries had attained the status of entrepreneurs on their own rights. Out of this 74.97 per cent were involved in Agricultural sector as landless labourer in the pre-project period.

The additional man-days generated as a result of shift in occupation works out of 56 lakh man-days. This would have generated about Rs. 1405.46 lakh income, for poor families outside IFAD project.

From a very modest saving of Rs. 2.3 lakh in 1990-91, the quantum of savings multiplied manifold within a period of seven years showing a quantum jump to Rs. 1423 lakh, which was far beyond the expectations of the project. Share of members savings to bank credit worked out to much higher at about 30.9 percent. Their march towards financial self-reliance was very effective and the goal of achieving uninterrupted credit cycles on their own is not far off if the savings are continued to be in tact. IFAD Project has built up the confidence in the formal credit agencies in the system and the members' access to it. Emphasis on promotion of self-reliance through self-managed group savings fund and group credit was paying dividends. The steep fall in the proportion of members taking recourse to moneylenders further reinforces this aspect.

Empowerment

More than 70 percent women feel that their self-confidence has considerably increased after joining the groups. Empowerment in terms of perceived respect from the family and society as a live experience for women was examined. The members perceived that about two-thirds of their husbands, relatives and neighbours had enhanced respect for the women members. Literacy of women is closely associated with their empowerment. Majority of the members were trained to sign their names. Women in Self-Help Groups were given training not only in income-generating activities but also to develop their other entitlements. About 83 percent of the beneficiaries attended Health and Nutrition Training programmes.

Women who changed their health and nutrition practices were preponderant (69% to 95%). About 56 per cent of the total women have adopted family planning methods.

The proportion of women having immunized their children ranged form 38 to 93 at Madurai and Salem districts respectively. Women of all five districts exhibited a high level of confidence in regard to sustaining family economically.

Collective and integrated activities of the Self-Help Groups are presumed to have helped them to get over the fears. SHG has helped majority of women to overcome their fears. 81 per cent from all districts opined that they got rid of their earlier fear complex while speaking with men. 75 per cent women express that they do not have fear now to talk with officials.

The percentage of women who would feel like protesting against various abuses ranged from 65 per cent to 70 per cent. This indicated that the SHG group activities have sensitized women to abuses that affront their dignity.

About 83 per cent of women are fully aware of their property rights. More than 80 percent were aware of the provision for women reservation in Panchayat. The same number of women had answered that no dowry could be demanded by men for their marriage with women. 76 per cent of women were in favour of widow remarriage. More than 94 per cent of the women were disapproving the practice of female infanticide. About 57 per cent women opined that the creation of federal structure for Self-Help Groups would be useful. 77 per cent of the women said that the banker's attitude had not changed towards poor women. 68 per cent of women members were aware of the federation of Self-Help Groups at Cluster level. Aware of Capital Development Fund (CDF) to the extent of 0 per cent, though they were not clear whether it was loan or grant. 93 per cent women had having absolute/good control over their income.

SHG women's participation in community services is an index of the political impact of collectivization on its members. The respondents have strengthened themselves in the context of family abuses. Member of SHG has worked in the cause of community development. Women members were largely involved in eight different types of community works. Resistance from families to the respondent's community activities had been very much less indicating that the whole family has been attuned to the group activities of women and also has given acceptance.

Readers of *Mutram* had gained knowledge pertaining to women-related issues. 56 percent of women are getting the magazine regularly. Almost 61 percent of the respondents read magazine *Mutram* regularly. 93 percent of women had absolute/good control over their income. More than 90 percent had positive attitude in helping other Self-Help Groups women.

Thus, the Self-Help Groups works have the best media for women empowerment.

4

Micro-Credit and Self-Help Group Women: Entrepreneurial Way of Empowering Rural Women

- Micro-Credit
- Emergence of Micro-Credit
- Micro-Credit and Economic Empowerment
- Women and Micro-Credit
- Micro-Finance and Self-Help Groups
- Micro-Credit and Economic Emancipation of Women

MICRO-CREDIT

"*Micro-credit is a critical anti-poverty tool—a wise investment in human capital. When the poorest, especially women, receive credit, they become economic actors with power. Power to improve not only their own lives but, in a widening circle of impact, the lives of their families, their communities, and their nations.*"

—Kofi Annan, Secretary General of the UN.

Micro-credit is the good choice to maximize utility and profit that encourage women's entrepreneurship. Household is considered as a unit of consumption. Women who choose exclusively in the household do so because both women and men recognize that women are better utilized in the home. Women receive lower wages outside and hence there is no total use of their resources. Women should be made to make their choice to utilize their full resources on par with men.

Entrepreneurship is viewed in general as an intensive human resource development. Entrepreneurs are those who start an economic activity on their own. As our agent of charge, the entrepreneur transforms physical, natural and human resources into productive possibilities. Human resources, both women and men of working age constitute the main strength of economic development of a nation. Women form an important segment of the labour force. The economic role played by them cannot be isolated from the work of development on the role and degree of economic integration of women is an indicator of women's independence and social status in general. The government is therefore making planned effort to include the spirit of enterprise among women through many incentives and developmental programmes. Entrepreneurship is the best avenue for mainstreaming women in the country's economic development because of certain factors. Emergence of entrepreneurship is considered to be closely linked to social, cultural, religious and psychological variables.

Micro-enterprises represent opportunities for self-employment which poor women, with appropriate support, can take advantage of. From the gender perspective, they represent an opportunity for women to gain direct access to income when they may have limited opportunity for women to gain direct access to income when they may have limited opportunities for alternative employment and in terms of economic empowerment, they provide scope for developing and exercising competence in managing an activity funds, taking responsibility for business transactions and taking decisions. The definition of micro-credit that was adopted by micro-credit summit 1997 as programmes extend small loans to very poor people for self-employment projects that generate income, allowing them to care for themselves and their families.

Micro-credit distinctly different from other populist poverty alleviation schemes. It must be understood that all small loans are not micro-finance. Micro-credit has some important features:

- Loans under micro-finance programmes are very small on an average less than $ 100 by world standards and in hundreds of rupees by Indian standards.

- Micro-credit continues to target the rural and urban households with emphasis on women borrowers, provision of finance for creation of assets and their maintenance and bringing in greater quality of service. Micro-finance providers themselves identify the beneficiaries independently of through VO's.
- Credit follows thrift. The first stage is the formation of groups by individuals themselves, followed by the mobilization of petty savings and recycling this by lending to group members.
- The repayment period is generally very short. The amount increases based on the borrower's repayment history. This is called the loan graduation process. The transactions are to be undertaken by mutual consent in truly informal manner.
- Loans are devoid of any concessionality and bear comparatively higher rate of interest. It is a significant departure from earlier exercises in providing credit to the poor through financial institutions at subsidized rates with high default rates.
- RBI has not imposed any minimum or maximum ceiling on the loan amount, assuming that the banks will be in a position to understand the underlying idea.
- The operational strategy of micro-credit involves very simple procedures for reviewing and approving loan applications, delivery of credit and related services at commercial rates of interest in a convenient and user-friendly way, quick disbursement of small and short-terms loans; clear recovery procedures and strategies; maintaining high repayment rates; incentives of access to larger loans immediately following successful repayment of first loan.
- Micro-credit focuses on the process retaining most of the earlier characteristics such as farm and non-farm credits, target groups being the poor, operating largely in rural and semi-urban areas and small borrower accounts. The new paragon emphasizes financial intermediation and self-sustainability of institutions and qualitative outreach to the poor.

EMERGENCE OF MICRO-CREDIT

The maximum experimentation with micro-credit can be seen in Bangladesh where it has been extensively used for reaching the poorest section of society. It has proved to be the most powerful weapon to fight poverty. During the seventies, many initiatives were taken in developed and developing countries in Asia, Africa and Latin America. The approach of micro-credit consisted of Self-Help Groups, Revolving Savings Credit Associations (ROSCAS), solidarity groups, money store, etc. Some of the examples outside India are ACCION International (Latin American Countries), Philippine Commercial and Industrial Bank, Rural Bank of Shana and Grameen Bank (Bangladesh). The Grameen Bank set-up in 1976 by Prof. Muhammad Yunus, is one of the most popular models of providing micro-credit to poor. At present, 90 percent of the members are women.

In our country, there is SEWA in Gujarat and Madhya Pradesh, MYRADA in Karnataka, PRADAN in Rajasthan, ASSEFA in Tamil Nadu, New Public School society in Uttar Pradesh, SAMBHAV in Madhya Pradesh and some other organiztions that took the initiative. The credit needs of groups are met in a convenient flexible and cost effective way.

NABARD's efforts of improving the access of the rural poor to formal banking services through Self-Help Groups gathered momentum during the last few years. It not only extends 100% refinance facilities to the banks at concessional interact rates, but it has also taken various promotional initiatives to expand SHG-Bank linkage programme. As a result, more than 2100 Self-Help Groups have been involved with the bank.

SIDBI also extends credit facilities through NGOs and more than 150 NGO's have availed credit facilities from SIDBI for lending to small borrowers.

Department of Women and Child Development launched the Indira Mahila Yojana (IMY) in 1995 as a Central Sector Project for the holistic empowerment of women in 200 blocks. Under this programme, efforts are being made for setting up of Self-Help Groups of women. The IMY aims to fill up the gaps where studies NGOs are not available to take up micro-credit programmes. The IMY has done a marvelous job in places such as Rohru Block of Shimla district.

Rashtriya Mahila Kosh (RMK) was set-up in March 1993 with the objective of extending credit limits to poor women through NGOs. Women Development Corporation (WDC), co-operative societies and Indira Mahila Block Samitees are taking up other promotional and advocacy roles to achieve economic self-reliance for women. Credit facilities are extended at 8% interest, which inturn is lent to Self-Help Groups at the interest rate of 12% per annum. Self-Help Groups can lend to women members at interest rate not exceeding the SBI interest rate on unsecured advances. NGOs can also extend loan facilities to individual women where Self-Help Groups do not exist.

Characteristics of Micro-Credit Programme

1. Targeting the very poor,
2. Simple procedures for reviewing and approving loan applications,
3. Delivery of credit and related services in a convenient and user-friendly way,
4. Quick disbursement of loans,
5. Clear recovery procedures and strategies,
6. Incentive of access to larger loans immediately following successful repayment of first loans,
7. Interest rates enough to cover the cost of operation,
8. Encouraging and accepting savings in concert with lending programmes,
9. Commitment to and training for, democratic participation in decision-making by all those involved as borrowers,
10. Tailoring Programme operations to reach women as recipients of micro-credit,
11. A system that can support sustained delivery to a significant and growing number of poor clients,
12. Accurate management and information systems that are actively used to make decisions motivate performance and provide accountability of management performance and the use of funds,
13. Micro-credit programme provides people with tools to achieve higher levels of economic independence and they encourage in widespread participation in organizational decision-making, and

14. Micro-credit programme organizes borrowers to bring them together to think through their common problems, agree on common issues, decide common action and forge common ideologies.

MICRO-CREDIT AND ECONOMIC EMPOWERMENT

Micro-credit was established as a mainstream development intervention even before the Beijing Platform for Action identified access to credit as a critical contributor to women's economic empowerment. Even before Muhammad Yunus, who started with an experimental project in Chittagong, established its Grameen Bank in 1983, several NGOs had taken up micro-credit as a central strategy. Fuelled by the World Bank—sponsored micro-credit summits, the credibility of micro-credit has grown to the point where it is being hailed as the ultimate answer to poverty and underdevelopment, to its proponents, micro-credit has everything—participation, flexibility, community ownership and, best of all, women's empowerment. To its critics, it is a Band-Aid solution to poverty, an easy way of side-stepping structural issues and making the poor responsible for finding solutions to their own problems.

In India, organization like SEWA in the early 1970s, and Annapurna Mahila Mandal and the Working Women's Forum in the 1980s, demonstrated the feasibility of small loans to poor women, primarily to support small entrepreneurial ventures. Today, almost every NGO worth the name runs a micro-credit programme, and major donors including the national financial institutions are involved. The World Bank has set a target of reaching 100 million of the world's poorest people with micro-credit by 2005, and has placed micro-credit at the center of its global strategy for poverty alleviation.

The micro-credit, approach is premised on some assumptions about the poor—that they are honest, that they do not shirk from repaying their debts, that they are willing to lend to each other and that they can assume responsibility for each other. The success of the approach has validated these assumptions many times over. Self-help groups of 15-20 persons, usually women are organized at the neighbourhood level. These groups meet regularly to save—usually small amounts of Rs. 5-10 a week—and circulate their savings as low-interest loans within the group whenever a member needs a loan.

Loans are usually taken for small enterprises, which, to judge from loan repayments, have a very high success rate. Repayment rates and terms are decided by the members and are highly context-specific. For most schemes, repayment rates are over 90%—far higher than the figures for formal banks. While each NGO has introduced minor variations (extensively documented as "best" practices), the basic outline of the approach is the same all over the world.

Discussions at a conference organized by six national women's organizations following the Global March 2000, and attended by representatives of over eighty grassroots women's groups and networks, reflected mixed feelings on the issue of microcredit.

On the one hand, most grassroots organizations were unequivocal in endorsing the strength of the "self-help" savings and credit movement of grassroots women. Millions of poor women, struggling to make a living through home-based enterprises or tiny initiatives in the informal sector, desperately need small amounts of credit to break their dependence on middlemen. The availability of credit without collateral on easy terms has enabled these enterprises to survive. Similarly, small loans from self-help groups for emergencies—doctor's bills, school fees, repair of huts, marriages—have helped women to escape from moneylenders. Every self-help group can cite instances where women have used loans to repay earlier loans taken from moneylenders and to redeem mortgaged assets.

Women's groups and NGOs also acknowledged the potential of microcredit as a platform for organization-building through intervention in the everyday struggles of poor women. The neighbourhood-based and decentralized mode of functioning of these groups is conducive to women's participation. Self-help groups have colonized spaces available to women within patriarchal social structure. Many self-help groups have moved beyond their initial agendas of savings and credit, to become genuine grassroots organizations, willing and able to take collective action to challenge vested interests.

However, national women's organizations also voiced their concern about the manner in which microcredit is being promoted as a panacea for poverty. It was pointed out that "success", for both government and NGOs, is gauged by the amount of money saved, the size and frequency of loans and the rate of loan repayment, rather than by the extent to which the economic exploitation of women has been reduced. There are practically no rigorous studies of changes in the income and expenditure patterns of members of SHG's before and after they take up economic activities using micro-credit. Similarly, there are very few studies that explore the extent to which micro-finance programmes have been able to facilitate non-economic dimensions of empowerment for women members of Self-Help Groups.

Organizations working with landless agricultural workers—who comprise the majority of poor women—have pointed out that their priorities are land and regular wage work, rather than setting up a micro-enterprise—in many cases, merely assuring payment of the minimum wage can result in doubling of the family income. Also, the success of micro-credit and micro-enterprise depends on a range of variables including market access, levels of family assets and risk-taking capacity—all of which exclude the "core" poor. Evaluations have confirmed that self-help groups tend to exclude the poorest women in any community, both because of their inability to save and because the other members see them as bad credit risks.

Women's organizations participation in the Global March 2000 linked the promotion of micro-credit and micro-enterprise projects by large multilateral and bilateral donors with their efforts to provide safety nets for women as part of the "human face" of globalisation. Organizations working with handloom weavers point out that, as part of the economic restructuring package, government is retreating from providing support in the form of subsidies on raw materials and marketing assistance to co-operatives of traditional artisans. Experience shows that this is precisely the support needed by Self-Help Groups, whether from the government or from a well-connected NGO. With government policies favouring the entry of multinationals into the rural market, these groups question the extent to which Self-Help Groups can provide a viable base for rural entrepreneurship.

Grassroots women's groups also expressed concern about the tendency of donors to piggyback their micro-finacne interventions on already existing groups, thus reducing costs and co-opting the work of smaller integrated programmes. In their eagerness to promote financially viable and minimalist interventions, donors are glossing over the contradiction emerging in micro-finance progammes, and are making unjustified assumptions about the "empowerment outcomes" of these programmes.

WOMEN AND MICRO-CREDIT

The micro-credit has particular relevance to women and their empowerment, considering the historical perspective of the involvement of women in the thrift and credit activity in the past there has been evaluation of local, informal credit structures.

To bridge the gap between the demand and supply of funds in the lower rungs of the rural economy, the formal sector took the initiative to develop a supplementary credit delivery mechanism by encouraging institutional arrangements outside the financial systems with the launching of NABARD's pilot scheme. Micro finance the development buzz word of the nineties to cure the illness of rural poverty gain visibility in the Indian development paragon has concepts like—reliance, self-sufficiency and self-help at its core. Targeting women for credit program began to receive serious considerations at the 1975 International World Conference in Mexico city. In India, this universal concern found recognition in South Plan, i.e. 1980-85. Since then, a concentrated efforts has been made in the direction by rural credit institutions, central and state governments.

Micro-credit as a system has fairly new approach. This is the concept of economic empowerment of women through the formation and nurturing of Self-Help Groups of the target population. Government has been conscious of developing and enabling policy environment in which the concern of women are reflected, articulated and redressed by government. To assist large number of weaker sections, meeting the credit needs of the poor asset less women, mostly in informal sector, banks have introduced novel approaches/innovations such as formation of Self-Help Groups of weaker sections, especially of women and inculcating in them the habit of regular saving and rotating the savings amongst them for productive as also non-productive purposes and thereby creating awareness for regular repayments.

Self-Help Groups are important components of micro-credit. A self-help group is a voluntary association of a homogenous association of a homogenous set of people, either working together or living in the neighborhood, engaged in similar line of activity, working with or without registration for the common good of the member.

MICRO-FINANCE AND SELF-HELP GROUPS

Micro-Finance scheme in India is dominated by Self-Help Groups. Based on the philosophy of group savings as collateral substitute, the SHG programme has been successful in not only designing financial products meeting peculiar needs of the poor, but also strengthening collective self-help capacities of the poor at the local level. The goal of Micro Finance System is to make it a dispenser not just of credit but of variety of social goods and services to the rural poor.

Micro-Finance Institutions (MFIs) are playing a major role in catering to the credit needs of the poorer sections of the rural society which banks in India were unable to do on their own. Micro-credit model was pioneered by the National Bank for Agriculture and Rural Development (NABARD) during 1991-92 has shown that establishing a linkage between an SHG and a bank is the best method for bringing Self-Help Groups into the ambit of formal banking especially because it infuses a degree of professionalism into the services offered to the rural poor.

The budget target of credit linking for 2005-06 from 2,00,000 self-help groups to 2,50,000. Commercial banks will be allowed to appoint MFIs as their "banking correspondents" for providing a variety of services of their behalf. 70 per cent of the rural poor do not have a bank account and 87 per cent do not have access to credit from a formal source. MFIs as agents for micro-insurance products will help spread the insurance habit and enable them to earn a fee income. Now the eligible MFIs can seek equity support from the redesignated Micro Finance Development and Equity Fund which has a corpus of Rs. 200 crore.

For the banking system, the SHG linkage has been a winning proposition, it is resulted in lower transaction costs, negligible defaults, and the generation of enormous goodwill. MFIs customized solutions based on their understanding of local conditions. Banks have not yet standardized their approach towards micro-lending. A lack of infrastructure and design facilities and also worthwhile distribution channels for marketing the products has constrained growth. At present 560 banks—48 commercial banks, 196 regional rural banks and 316 co-operative banks—are actively involved in the programme. Originally confined to Andhra Pradesh, Tamil Nadu, Pondicherry and Karnataka, MFIs are now spreading to the rest of the country. India has the world's most extensive banking infrastructure. Today, there are about 60,000 retail credit outlets of the formal banking sector comprising 12,000 branches of district level cooperative banks. Over 14,000 branches of the Regional Rural Banks (RRBs) and over 30,000 rural and semi-urban branches of commercial banks; in addition to 1,12,000 co-operative credit societies at the village level.

There are few empirical studies to prove the commercial Viability and the comparative product strength of Self-Help Groups in banks credit portfolios. Until rigorous and extensive studies are completed, the jury remains out on the sustainability of both the Self-Help Groups and of the SHG-bank linkage model for the banks delivering it.

The Indian micro-finance sector reflects many of the key successes and remaining challenges common round the globe:

- A wide range of financial institutions offer a variety of financial services to the poor.
- The diversity of settings and the different levels of political, social and economic development necessitate this variety of institutional types adapted to the local context.
- Liberalized interest rates are necessary to allow/encourage banks and MFIs to serve their low income customers on a sustainable basis because of the high volume of low value transactions involved. But India's proves in information technology should allow it to lead the world in the development of e-banking solutions for the poor.
- The unparalleled banking infrastructure in India offers a significant opportunity to accelerate, deepen and improve the quality of access to financial services for the poor, and to develop an inclusive, sustainable financial system.
- There is a growing recognition that lack of human capacity remains one of the key barriers to developing full-fledged inclusive, sustainable financial system.

Advantages

- Since banks can extend their coverage at far lower costs than would be possible with their own networks. The MFIs would gain by handling a variety of sophisticated financial products and earn a fee income, they will also come under the discipline of the more regulated banking sector.
- For the banking system the SHG linkage has been a winning proposition. It has resulted in lower transaction costs, negligible defaults and the generation of enormous goodwill. The MFIs would be able to provide customized solutions based on their understanding of local conditions.

Micro-finance is gathering momentum to become a major force in India. The Self-Help Group (SHG) model with bank lending to groups of poor women without collateral has become an accepted part of rural finance. With traditionally loss-making rural banks shifting their portfolio away form the rural poor in the post-reform period, SGG-based micro-finance, nurtured and aided by NGOs, have become an important alternative to traditional lending in terms of reaching the poor without incurring a fortune in operating and monitoring costs. The government and NABARD have recognized this and have emphasized the SHG approach and working along with NGOs in its initiatives. Over half a million Self-Help Groups have been linked to banks over the years but a handful of states, mostly in South India, account for over three-fourth of this figure with Andhra Pradesh being an undisputed leader. In spite of the impressive figures, micro-finance in India is still presently too small to create a massive impact in poverty alleviation, but if pursued with skill and opportunity development of the poor, it holds the promise to alter the socio-economic face of the India's poor.

Ensuing women's a micro-credit through schemes is a major component of strategies both for poverty reduction and women's empowerment. Throughout the country, thousand of women's Self-Help Groups have been formed through government programmes such as Rashtriya Mahila Khosh (RMK), IFAD, SGSY, SHSRY, Mahalir Thittam—Tamilnadu Corporation for Development of Women Ltd. At present, micro-credit through women Self-Help Groups has become a central desent of the development vision. Micro-credit works when other empowerment strategies are as part of social transformation. These strategies have included assisting women to have increased control over their incomes and resources, helping women to define their own priorities, and ensuing their participation in decision-making at various levels Productive role, Reproductive role and community managing role. Micro-credit empowers women since it accords economic independence and builds confidence by virtue of their participation in groups and its activities.

Women have been of their economic status, especially in rural areas. The empowerment of women and of their status and economic role needs to be integrated into economic development programmes. Rural women, especially those who are below poverty line and grass-root level have limited access to resources and regular employment choices that would make them financially independent. The women suffer a lot even to fulfil the basic minimum consumption needs.

The IFAD programme was taken up in Tamil Nadu from 1989-90 onwards with assistance. Women were organized in Self-Help Groups to undertake both social and economic development activities.

Little money goes a long way...

In Bangladesh, Grameen Bank the micro finance has been served as a most powerful weapon to. The self-help groups associated closely with micro-credit systems, the activities of the groups have emerged as a sustainable approach to make credit flexibilities to the poor at their door steps in a simple manner. Micro-credit programmes provided the services to the poor women for their income generating activities and enabling them to take care of themselves and their families.

The concept of micro-credit or lending small amounts of money to groups that are excluded by the conventional banking system can help China in its quest to build a harmonious society, according to Grameen Bank founder and winner of the 2006 Nobel Peace Prize, Muhammad Yunus.

Explaining the difference between conventional banks and micro-credit, the Nobel laureate said, "In conventional banks the more you have, the more you can get, whereas in micro-credit the less you have, the more priority you get. His pioneering Grameen Bank requires no collateral at all from borrowers." "The idea is to turn conventional banking on its head, so we don't go into a borrower's past at all. We run no credit checks and absolutely no one is excluded even those with a criminal record are welcomed," he explained.

It is with great delight that we learn of the Nobel Foundation's decision to award the Nobel Peace Prize for 2006 to Grameen Bank and its founder, Prof. Muhammad Yunus. The prize was awarded to Grameen Bank's "efforts to create economic and social development from below". A Press Release from the Nobel Foundation announced on 13 October 2006 that "Lasting peace can not be achieved unless large population groups find ways in which to break out of poverty. Micro-credit is one such means development from below also serves to advance democracy and human rights."

The set-up the Grameen Bank in 1976 to give credit to poor people in his country, particularly women, in order to let them set-up micro businesses without collateral. During the 1970s Muhammad Yunus discovered by loaning small amounts of money to the poor—amounts too minute for banks to take any interest—he could empower the poverty stricken to build small businesses. This revolution in poverty alleviation became to be known as Micro-enterprise, and today has benefited millions of people around the world.

Professor Yunus credits the Grameen bank's amazing recovery rate of 98 percent to the fact that the entire system is based on trust. "We put our trust in the borrowers; in people that the rest of society has written off and in return they want to honour that trust." (*The Hindu*, 26 October 2006)

Micro-Credit System

The micro-credit contributes not only to poverty alleviation, but also the empowerment of poor trodden people. The strategy of micro-credit directly provides the economic benefits, indirectly helps for social empowerment. The micro-finance interventions make charges in improving the status of women, self-confidence and self-reliance. Though the micro-credit has different models. A common feature has been the promotion of self-help groups through social mobilization, composed mainly of women, which start with pooled savings for internal rotation, and eventually receive and repay loans. NGOs, government agencies and banks have been promoting Self-

Help Groups, within three broad approaches. In the first approach, micro-credit is seen as an entry point or complementary activity to mobilize people and sustain interest, though the principal objective is something else such as promoting literacy and education, enhancing maternal and child health, facilitating watershed development, catalyzing women's empowerment, or reducing child labour. In the second approach, micro-finance is used as the main tool for poverty alleviation. The nation-wide, centrally sponsored Swarnajayanti Gram Swarozgar Yojana (SGSY) scheme is a notable example, apart from programmes of several NGOs. In the third approach, the relative strengths of the government, NGOs and banks are sought to be combined under an umbrella organization promoting multi-purpose Self-Help Groups, where micro-finance is an input along with systematic training and capacity building in virtually any subject of concern and interest to the members. One example is the Tamil Nadu Women's Development Project called Mahalir Thittam (Anuradha Rajiwan, 2005).

Self-Help groups has emerged has the important mechanism in the process of participatory and empowerment and due to socio-economic and science the rural women are marginalized in the society to improve their status in the self-help group serves as a ladder. Poverty is a major problem for survival, but self-help groups are forming in a level and serves as lighthouse to meet their immediate financial requirement. Each member saves in small amount periodically after sometime self-serving amounted will become a sizable amount in that paying borrow money for their livelihood. After sometime as it as have tie up with financial institutions like banks to a wide external finance and they well dead loans from them for investment for their income activities.

Micro-credit initiate, increase and sustained the process of economic development in the following ways:

- Improvement in per capita income.
- Improvement of living standard.
- Economic Independence.

Micro-credit serves as the solution of Self-Help Groups to enable the rural poor women for their economic empowerment and sustainable livelihood. The Self-Help Groups are very flexible and democratic in functioning and exist method of economy to have income governing activities. This micro-credit strategy offers the opportunity to the rural poor women to serve rightful phase in the rural economy in the right time.

Ensuring women's access to credit through micro-credit schemes is a major component of strategies both for poverty induction and women's empowerment. Throughout the country, thousands of women's Self-Help Groups have been formed through Government Programmes such as Rashtriya Mahila Kosh (RMK), SGSY, SGSRY, Mahalir Thittam (Tamilnadu Corporation for Development of Women Ltd.). At present, Micro-credit through women's Self-Help Groups has become a Central element of the development vision.

Micro-credit works when other empowerment strategies are as part of social transformation. These strategies have included arising women to have increased control over their incomes and resources, helping women to define their own priorities, and ensuring their participation in decision-making at various levels, Productive role, Reproductive role and community managing role. Micro-credit serves as a tool for poverty alleviation and empowerment. Micro-credit empowers women since it accords economic independence and builds confidence by virtue of their participation in groups and its activities. The Micro-Finance movement is the appropriate solution to the attack on poverty. The concerns strategy of Bank, Bangladesh inspired on the institution working for poverty.

Hillary Clinton wrote, "Micro-enterprise is the heart of development because micro-enterprise programmes work—they lift women and families out of poverty. It is called micro but it's effect on the people is macro; we have seen that it takes just a few dollars, often as little as 10 to help a woman gain self-employment to lift her and her family out of poverty. It is not a handout: it is a helping hand." (Kaladhar, 1997).

Linda Mayouz identified that micro-finance helps in: (i) "increasing women's income levels and control over income leading to greater level of economic independence. (ii) Access to networks and markets giving wider experience of the world outside the home, access to information and possibilities of development of other social and political roles. (iii) Enhancing perceptions of women's contributions to household income and family welfare, increasing women's participation in household decisions about expenditure and other issues and leading to greater expenditure for women's welfare" (Mayouz, 2000).

MICRO-CREDIT AND ECONOMIC EMANCIPATION OF WOMEN

Various case studies show that there is a positive correlation between micro-credit and women empowerment.

Anuradha Rajiwan conducted a case study in Share Micro-finance Limited (SML) in Andhra Pradesh to know to what extent, micro-finance interventions, when used as tools for poverty alleviation, impact on women's empowerment.

SML's experiences with micro-finance demonstrate that this primarily credit-for-income generation-based model of small women's groups, well-oriented in receiving and repaying loans, closely supervised with trained staff does lead to significant, first-level improvements in the individual lives of members and their households, in contrast to non-members or new members. There are also some beginnings of change in the position and status of women's groups as collectives. In respect of the wider socio-economic environment, changes are observed in respect to dependence on money-lenders, poverty profiles in villages, and a greater willingness to retain children, especially girls, in full-time education. The changes are all considered positive by women as well as men. These developments are taking place in the absence of systematic capacity building on gender or women's empowerment issues. The nature of facilitation for social mobilization and capacity building of group members itself influences the range and extent of empowerment, no less than credit. The potential for change seems to be greater than what has been actualized so far.

There are increases in incomes and assets in the hands of poor women, which is a significant improvement over their pre-membership situation. The benefits from this increase flow to the household as a whole. Other family members, in particular husbands, well appreciate women contributing more money to the household on a regular basis. Consequently, other non-income benefits to women like changes in personality, greater self-confidence and greater say within and outside the house are not resisted.

The consistent 100 per cent repayment rates have not only

enabled women to access repeat loans, but also enabled women to be able to rely on repeat loans. Moreover, high rates of repayment combined with prudent cost consciousness has made SML's operations sustainable in the long-run. It also makes SML an attractive investment destination for commercial financial institutions, enabling greater resource flow in future.

However, loan sizes are currently small, restricting further growth of businesses. SML is aware of this and in the process of experimenting with larger small enterprise loans for members who have a long and sound repayment history. Technical skill training to improve existing skills and to learn new skills in absent and most women restrict their businesses to what they already know and to local markets. There is no support for strengthening marketing through expanding skills in sales, design, modern packaging, branding, standardization and quality control. These factors also limit business and income growth. Because of the sharply focused objectives of SML and its concern with costs, such support is currently outside their agenda.

Women have greater control over their resources—assets, earnings and savings. A husband cannot sell the asset acquired on the basis of a loan from SML, except with the woman's consent. Women have a greater say in household expenditure, arising directly from their contributions. They are spending on gas stoves and fans that reduce the drudgery of domestic work and thus improve quality of life of family members. However, other independent expenditure on themselves, though more than before, tends to be small, restricted to saris and bangles, with most of their money being used for the benefit of the household or for improving their micro-businesses. For major expenses, women consult their husbands. However, the reverse is true too: now husbands also consult their wives more often than earlier.

A significant change is the transformation of women from low-wage workers to owner—managers. This is widely valued not only because of higher income prospects, but also due to a perceived increase in dignity and control. This change is associated with less time spent in hard labour as well as, in some cases, more time spent on the new work situation. However, more time spent on work is seen as resulting in more returns, and therefore liked by them.

There is an increased cooperation between husbands and wives.

While husbands have not started helping in any significant way in unpaid domestic work, they have started helping in their wives' business-related work, especially where the businesses are thriving. Some have even given up their own occupations to join their wives on a full-time basis. While this is seen as beneficial, whether this could eventually lead to a lessening of control by women is not as yet clear. However, women's access to credit, combined with self-confidence, is a countervailing factor, helping to keep control with women. Moreover, SML itself would like to see women retain control so that repayments are not adversely affected. This congruence of interest between SML and members contributes to the first level of women's empowerment.

Increased incomes have resulted in very visible increases in self-confidence and self-worth. Women volunteer to give their opinions, are more articulate, can negotiate better within their households, can present their demands to government officials without hesitation, and can ask questions and demand information. Many reports picking up new ideas from the television. Women's mobility has increased and they travel more freely. Other family members consider it legitimate that women stay out late in connection with group meetings or business. But women are not yet commonly riding mopeds and bicycles (as is observed in Maharashtra and parts of Tamil Nadu). Travelling or staying out late for other reasons like tourism or pilgrimage is not reported.

While domestic violence is not eliminated, women members report a decrease, combined with their increased ability to cope with it. They relate this to their increased economic worth. Birth control is almost universally practiced, especially among the younger generation. This is more a trend effect, rather than one arising out of group membership. Women are discussing contraception issues with their husbands. While there is a desire for small family size with one or two children, there is still a preference for a male child. Women undergo terminal methods of birth control after the couple has attempted to have a son, often resulting in family sizes larger than desired. Male sterilization is rare, even though simpler and less expensive. However, simultaneously, there is an increase in the value of girls. Younger daughters are more likely to remain in school for longer periods and married later. Increased value for daughters is related to group membership.

As groups, the local village communities have started to recognize women's collectives. They are regarded not only as important sources of credit access and incomes, but also as tools to approach officials and articulate village needs. However, the picture on political/democratic empowerment is mixed. SML, of course, does not concern itself with orienting women on these issues. Voting is near universal, regardless of group membership. While a majority of members seem to be voting as per their own decisions, there are examples of members voting as per instructions of husbands. A far larger number of women are standing as candidates for elections to local bodies than before. While this is primarily a result of reservations for women, rather than group membership, the effect of SML is seen in the quality of candidature. More 'genuine' women candidates are reported to come from out of group members and real contests are reported from constituencies where members have stood. But there is very limited participation in the grama sabhas. Most members reported that they did not even know when the grama sabhas were conducted or what was to be discussed in them. The groups are not yet a democratic force and wooing for votes takes place more on a community basis.

Government agencies and banks do not recognize SML groups for linkages and benefits, perhaps due to SML itself being independent of government, a bank substitute. SML does not facilitate these linkages. The groups see SML as a bank, popularly calling it 'SHARE Bank'. However, in individual cases members are accessing benefits from government schemes. SML is open about this and does not inhibit them from availing these benefits. Some groups have been successful in placing their needs before the relevant authorities and getting them addressed. Such linkages could be more systematically facilitated at group/center levels in sectors where there is no competition or conflict of approach, for example, for improved access to and a say in the operation of health centers, ICDS services, PDS, water supply, sanitation, education for girls, etc., rather than with SGSY or NABARD's SHG-bank linkage programme.

Changes in the wider socio-economic environment are more significant than changes in groups. There is a sharp reduction in dependence on moneylenders among member households, especially after the second year. The rural economy is getting more diversified as members take to a variety of economic activities. Growth of the service sector is observed. These developments help in combating seasonality factors and business risks, contributing to a widening and deepening of the rural economy. Poverty profiles are changing. More WHHs derive economic and social benefits of group membership. More widows and abandoned women enjoy greater security. However, while SML aims to target poor women, there are also cases where member orientation has not focused on this, resulting in the exclusion of the worst-off as they are seen as unable to cope with weekly repayments. Diet patterns have improved with consumption of a variety of purchased vegetables and fruits (as against gathered leaves with rice and rotis) and weekly consumption of meat. With an increase in market-oriented work for women, a possible temptation to utilize the help of children to earn more can arise, adversely affecting their attendance and enrolment in schools. But this is not in fact observed. Members are more aware of the value of education, including for girls. It is husbands who are helping out more than children. Children do help, but not during school hours.

The changes that are taking place flow from the joint facilitation of group strengthening with credit access for women, rather than from credit access *per se*. Moreover, the nature of social mobilization and the kind of capacity building that takes place in the process of group formation seems to be just as important in influencing the type and extent of women's empowerment. SML's focus being primarily credit-based for income generation and poverty reduction, there are limitations to the range and extent of empowerment that can be reasonably expected to take place 'incidentally'. Certain changes are not part of SML's agenda like orientation of women on gender and women's empowerment, orientation of men and building in them skills to cope with changing male-female relationships, deeping democratic participation, and enabling women to address not just their practical needs but also their strategic interests. Hence, it would not be fair to expect them to have taken place.

The conclusion here is that a very good triggering-off for women's empowerment has taken place with a strong economic foundation, and a precondition for further change has been established. Now the time is ripe for more explicit strategy to widen the scope of women's empowerment. Awareness building on gender and empowerment among, both the facilitators and members of micro-finance can help counter historical, patriarchal, socio-cultural and political factors, which prevent women and men from growing up to their full potential and supplementing SML's economic inputs. It is not necessary that this awareness generation be funded by SML. Alternatives could be considered. For example, SML could consider linking up with other relevant agencies and individual specialists on gender for building capacity in this area. SHARE Society itself could work in tandem with SML or set-up another wing within the SHARE group. There does not have to be a contradiction between a primarily credit-based and primarily other-than-credit-based approach, as each has the potential to strengthen the other, forging a symbiotic relationship. (Anuradha Rajiwan, 2005).

Samirendra Nath Dhar had a study on poverty alleviation and women empowerment through the synergistic endeavours of micro finance in North Bengal. Development of micro-enterprises in this area and putting thrust on alleviation of poverty can go a long way in sustainable socio-economic development of this region. The main objective of the study is to know the economic and social activities carried out by Self-Help Groups, to the impact of Self-Help Groups on the socio-economic rights and of women in this region and to assess the problems faced by women in Self-Help Groups regarding execution of their micro-entrepreneurial activities. In his findings he highlighted that from a more 767 groups in the year 2000 the number of groups have to about 21,000 groups a span of five years, showing a growth rate of more than 27 times. This substantial number of groups has been emerged in a short span of time by NGOs and DRDC with the help of local self-governments and commercial or regional rural banks. The economic activities of the Self-Help Groups range from spice-making, dairy and poultry, stone crushing, mushroom, jute products, pin apple, cultivation, tailoring and coloured fish, this analysis reveals that though social and economic benefits and rights have accrued to the beneficiaries, yet the degree of economic benefits is not very appreciate. Therefore, an attempt was made to measure the perception of problems faced by the women and solutions were suggested like increasing the number of basic orientation training programmes, and to ensure better understanding and co-ordinations between the bank officials, functions of DRDC's and SHG promoting institutions. The findings of the study have demonstrated that the efforts taken for poverty alleviation through self-employment-based micro-finance programme has to some extent been able to synergistically deliver greater socio-economic rights and powers to the beneficiaries. (Anil Bhuimali, 2005)

Hari Srinivas pointed out that micro-credit is the extension of small loans to entrepreneurs too poor to qualify for traditional bank loans. It has proven an effective and popular measure in the on going struggle against poverty, enabling those without access to lending institutions to borrow at bank rates, and start small business.

The key implications of micro-credit are in its name itself: 'micro'. A number of issues come to mind when 'micro' is considered: The small size of the loans made, small size of savings made, the smaller frequency of loans, shorter repayment periods and amounts, the micro/local level of activities, the community-based immediacy of micro-credit, etc. Hence, micro-credit is not the solution, but is a menu of options and enablements, that has to be put together, based on local conditions and needs.

With the current explosion of interest on micro-credit issues, several developmental objectives have come to be associated with it, besides that of only "credit". Of particular importance is savings—as an end in itself, and as a guarantee for loans. Micro-credit has been used as an 'inducer' in many other community development activities, used as an entry point in a community organizing programme and as an ingredient in larger education/training exercises.

An interesting stand is taken by the Virtual Library on Micro-credit itself—it takes micro-credit beyond the confines of 'money' and declares in its conceptual framework that—

> "Micro-credit" is as much about *money* as it is about information. With sustainability and non-dependence on external resources being key to the growth of micro-credit programmes, the Homepage focuses on providing pertinent and timely information in the form of strategies, tools, ideas and guides, to grassroots and intermediary organizations, and at the same time, educating the larger public on broader issues related to micro-finance and micro-credit.

The Centre for Women's Studies, Alagappa University, Karaikudi, Tamil Nadu conducted a research on Impact of Self-Help Group on Women Empowerment with special focus on micro-credit.

Background

The Centre for Women's Studies of Alagappa University was established in 1989 at Karaikudi. The activities and programmes of CWS were designed to help achieve for these women, equal participation, self-reliance, socio-economic independence, a positive self-image, and a quality life. This challenging task demanded the Centre to have a very large commitment, intense and arduous work, a continuous search for new alternatives, multi-pronged activities and concerted efforts of all categories of people—academics, social activists, government officials and the women themselves.

The activities of the Centre are directed to improve the situation and status of women at all levels. Participation of both men and women and collaboration of different agencies and sectors are encouraged. The activities are channeled through—

- Teaching and Training
- Research
- Extension
- Dissemination (Library, Documentation and Publication)
- Advocacy
- Seminars and Workshops
- Networking and Co-ordinating
- Monitoring and Review

Area of Operation and Growth

The area of operation of CWS includes the district of Sivaganga. The activities of CWS concentrate Sakkottai Union in Karaikudi Municipality. Over a period of Seventeen years, CWS has been successful in building up a large administrative infrastructure and reaching out to the rural poor in the backward areas within Sivaganga District. Because of its' involvement in multi-faceted activities, several funding agencies at the national and international level have shown interest and confidence in CWS. The Centre has organised more than 200 Awareness Programmes. Thus, CWS has recorded a phenomenal growth for the past seventeen years.

Women Centered Activities

Centre for Women's Studies has implemented several activities. CWS has been instrumental in organizing rural women to show their

Objectives	*Strategies*
To examine the diverse aspects of the lives of women and develop a critical and balanced understanding of their position and potentials in society.	Research Awaerness Programmes Interaction and Dialogue with concerned women groups Seminar/Workshops/Symposia Field work
To empower Women with self-employment Possibilities, inculcate in them entrepreneurial concepts and skills, and open avenues for economic independence.	Self-employment Training Science and Technology workshops and Training Entrepreneurship Development Programmes
To promote development of women in terms of career goals, decision-making and effective life options.	Training in Leadership and Career Choices Training in Decision-making and political participation Village camps with people participation, Formation of Self-help women groups in villages.
To incorporate knowledge about the relevance of Women's Studies in the established disciplines of the University.	Curriculum designing and counseling to the Universities and colleges in starting Courses in Women's Studies. Producing relevant Teaching/Learning Materials Seminars/Workshops/Symposia
To encourage researches that will generate knowledge of Women's studies, role and contributions in family and society, and programmes on women.	Action-oriented Researches Field Projects Evaluation Studies
To introduce new perspectives, frame-work and tools of analysis for inter-disciplinary work.	Guest Lectures/Seminars/Workshops on interdisciplinary basis.
To reach out to rural women in order to enhance their status through productive employment and ensure their participation in an integrated development process with greater awareness of their roles, rights, and potentials.	Adoption of villages Camps/Workshops/Training courses for village girls and women Networking with women groups and establish linkages with Governmental and Non-Governmental Agencies

strength and defend themselves for their rights with the formation of Mahalir Thittam. The Centre has been an active agent in forming, counselling, training and evaluating Self-Help Groups under Mahalir Thittam of Tamilnadu Government.

For women to get gainful employment especially belonging to SC, ST and BCs. Self-help groups were formed under Swarnajayanthi Gram Swarozgar Yojana (SGSY) Scheme in collaboration with District Rural Development Agency, Sivaganga. The Centre so far formed 70 groups under SGSY Scheme. The Centre conduct training programmes for the office-bearers help in getting loans and give skill training.

Growth and Performance of Self-Help Groups

The successful working of Mahalir Thittam has resulted in the formation of a large number of Self-Help Groups. The centre has been an active agent in forming, counselling, training and evaluating Self-Help Groups under Mahalir Thittam of Tamilnadu Government, the Centre was chosen as the first University Centre to work in Sakkottai block of Sivaganga District. In 1989 with the help from CWS, 600 Self-Help Groups were formed involving 15-17 women members and the total membership of 10,200. The significant feature of this system was that a large number of women shifted their borrowing from traditional moneylenders to Self-Help Groups. CWS has arranged about Rs. 8 crores from banks. Some of the notable features of this scheme are a high percentage (100) of payment, utilization of funds for income creating activities and generation of saving by women members in the Self-Help Groups.

Overall Micro-Credit

- Nearly 90% of the respondents have relieved from fulltime household activities and engaged in Income Generating Activities both agriculture and non-agricultural trades.
- Improvement in the income levels of Self-Help Groups members.
- Nearly 100% recovery of loans.
- Maintenance of Proper accounts by the Self-Help Groups.
- More than 80% of the respondents are aware of Mahalir Thittam schemes Swarna Jayanthi Gram Swarojgar Scheme, Prime Minister Rozgar Yojana Scheme (PMRY), 5 lakh

women Entrepreneurship Development Programme (EDP) and Sarva Shiksha Abiyan.

- Majority of the respondents were aware of the magazine 'Mutram' and stated that they gained the knowledge pertaining to women-related issues.
- More than 90% of the respondents have engaged in Income Generating Activities such as animal husbandry, agriculture, grocery shop, tailoring, petty trade, mushroom cultivation, manufacturing of washing materials.
- Most 90% of the respondents lead a decent joyful life and 40% of the respondents have shifted their profession from housewife to entrepreneurs.
- Nearly 70% of the respondents have undergone EDP training and started an Income generating activities.
- 90% of the respondents felt that their earnings were useful to family. Some of the family expenses were met by the Sangah loan availed through groups.
- 56% of the respondents said that they have absolute control over their income.
- The SHG members have won the confidence on decision-making regarding children's education, freedom to express views of opinion at home, decision on household expenses and transacting with bankers and going alone for any business.

Thus, the micro-credit serves as an important tool to fulfil the objective of strategic gender needs and make women active participant for economic emancipation.

Self-Help Group and Human Resource Development

- Human Resource Development
- Women and Human Resource Development
- Capabilities Approach
- Human Development Index
- Women Empowerment, Human Resource Development and Sustainable Development

HUMAN RESOURCE DEVELOPMENT

Human development is a process of enlarging people's choices. Enlarging people's choices is achieved by expanding human capabilities and functioning. At all levels of development the three essential capabilities for human development are for people to lead long and healthy lives, to be knowledgeable and to have access to the resources needed for a decent standard of living. If these basic capabilities are not achieved, many choices are simply not available and many opportunities remain inaccessible. But the realm of human development goes further: essential areas of choice, highly valued by people, range from political, economic and social opportunities for being creative and productive to enjoying self-respect, empowerment and a sense of belonging to a community.

Income is certainly one of the main means of expanding choices and well-being. But it is not the sum total of people's lives.

Jan Nederveen Pieterse in his work on Development Theory says that human development makes a strong case for combining equity and growth along the lines of human capital, but leaves the social dimension unexplored. The human development (HD) perspective takes the further step of making a general case for the nexus between equity and growth. According to Keith Griffin, 'under some circumstances, the greater is the degree of equality, the faster is likely to be the rate of growth'. His considerations include the cost of the perpetuation of inequality and that inequality undermines political legitimacy while 'modern technology has destroyed the monopoly of the state over the means of violence'. Furthermore, 'measures to reduce inequality can simultaneously contribute to faster growth'. Further elements mentioned by Griffin are investments in education—'There is probably no easier way to combine equality and rapid growth. The whole of East Asia is testimony to the veracity of this proposition'—and the liberation of women. 'A final example of the falsity of the great trade-off is the liberation of women. Equal treatment of women would release the talent, energy, creativity and imagination of half the population' (Buvini *et al.*, 1996).

A broadly similar case is made by Ul Haq, who mentions 'four ways to create desirable links between economic growth and human development': investment in education, health and skills; more equitable distribution of income; government social spending; and empowerment of people, especially women. Ul Haq proposes a HD paradigm of equity, sustainability, productivity, and empowerment (Jan Nederveen Pieterse, 2004).

Global Concern and Human Development

Here is how human development relates to current global concerns:

Human Rights. Human development leads to the realization of human rights—economic, social, cultural, civil and political. The human development perspective takes an integrated view of all human rights—not the narrow and exclusive focus on civil and political rights. It provides a framework in which advancing human development is commensurate with realizing human rights.

The1948 Universal Declaration of Human Rights affirms that "everyone has the right to a standard of living adequate for the health and well-being of himself and his family, including food, clothing, housing and medical care and necessary social services... Everyone has the right... to education... to work... [and] to social security." Subsequent international human rights instruments reaffirmed people-centred development as a universal right—identifying as additional dimensions the right to security, participation, freedom of association, freedom from discrimination and exclusion from development.

Collective well-being. Individual rights, choices and opportunities cannot, however, be unlimited. One person's freedom can constrain or violate the freedom of many other. As the reaction to the excessive individualism of the free market shows, there is a need for socially responsible forms of development. Individual and collective well-being are interwined, and human development requires strong social cohesion and equitable distribution of the benefits of progress to avoid tension between the two. And the power of collective action is an essential driving force in the pursuit of human development.

Equity. Concerns for equity take centre stage in the human development perspective. The notion of equity is most often applied to wealth or income. But human development emphasizes equity in basic capabilities and opportunities for all-equity in access to education, in health, in political rights.

Sustainability. Sustainability means meeting the needs of present generations without compromising the abilities and opportunities of future generations. It thus implies both intra-generational and inter-generational equity. Sustainability is an important dimension of human development. Human development is a process of enlarging people's choices. But such enhancement must be for both present and future generations without sacrificing one for the other.

In the 1990s there have been major global debates on sustainable development (United Nations Conference on Environment and Development in Rio, 1992) and for people-centred sustainable development (World Summit for Social Development in Copenhagen, 1995). These have a common core, not to be missed, with human development. Human development is not a concept separate from sustainable development—but it can help to rescue "sustainable development" from the misconception that it involves only the environmental dimension of development. All these approaches have emphasized the need for people-centred development, with concerns for human empowerment, participation, gender equality, equitable growth, poverty reduction and long-term sustainability. (Human Development Report, 1998)

WOMEN AND HUMAN RESOURCE DEVELOPMENT

As discussed by T.V. Rao, Human Resource Development has many facets of development of people including their physical, intellectual and emotional, social, moral, political, sprititual and all other forms of development. Human Resource development implies that people may be developed individually, or as groups or as communities and collectives. When an individual acquires capabilities, they enable the individual to make things happen. However, societies are much more than individuals. They are required to function as groups and they may also be grouped into collectives, for example, the poor or landless are a collective of people who are poor and without land; some of them may organize themselves to form action groups.

Human Resource Development looks at the process of developing such groups and collectives to function better or transform themselves by acquiring new competencies. Some of the groups in a country have a strategic significance due to the multiplier effect their development has on others. Women self-help group which is important because of the multiplier effect they have on the development of others through families. Women have been found to influence social, economical, educational and well-being of the entire family and villages.

Approaches to Human Resource Development

There were three distinct approaches to human resource development in 1960s and 70s; human capital-oriented social psychology-based and poverty-driven represented by Shultz and Mcchelland. But at present women empowerment approach surely leads to high growth of human development index of India.

The women empowerment emphasizes equity in basic capabilities and opportunities for all-equity in the three basic dimensions of human development—longevity, knowledge and descent standard of living. Women are in important position in human resource development. Primarily they are the producers of the future young generation. The education status of women brings benefits not only the family but also the whole society. Hence, the social, economic and political empowerment of women will have a good impact on human resource development. T.V. Rao pointed out that no country or society can achieve its potential without adequately inviting in developing the capabilities of women and encouraging the empowerment of women. Human resource development involves women. It requires that the capabilities of women be improved, that disadvantages and discrimination be removed and that the women have the opportunity to become active participants in all aspects of society. Empowering women is a key element in the success of human resource development programme. He suggested the following strategies could be used to empower women: Educating girls and women, facilitating their involvement in economic activity through development of their entrepreneurial and income earning capabilities and access to credit, involving women in policy formulation and decision-making, encouraging socio-cultural change by exploring gender issues and promoting the effective implementation of equal rights legislation.

CAPABILITIES APPROACH

> "The conception (Aristotelian social democracy) does not aim directly at producing people who function in certain ways. It aims, instead, at producing people who are capable of functioning in these ways; who have both the training and the resources to so function, should they choose. The choice itself is left to them. And one of the capabilities Aristotelian government most centrally promotes is the capability of choosing; of doing all these functions in accordance with one's own practical reason. The government aims at capabilities, and leaves the rest to the citizens."
>
> —*Martha C. Nussbaum*

Development starts and ends with people. For a country's advancement, nothing is stronger, richer and more generative than human resource. Capabilities approach deals with the capabilities and needs that join all humans, across barriers of gender, class, race and nation. Capabilities are privileges that all humans share and not those which enhance the power and status of any dominant group.

The focus on what is common to all is contrary to the gender ideology that divides and discriminates women and women. Capabilities can be understood as basic capabilities and high level capabilities. Basic capabilities are the low-level capabilities required for the shape of the human form of life. To consider one as a human being, the person must share with other human beings the capability of mortality; human body—capable of hunger and thirst and, therefore, feels the need for food and drink need for shelter, sexual desire and mobility—capability for pleasure and pain; cognitive capacity; early infant development; practical reason; affiliation with other human beings; relatedness to other species and nature; humour and play; separateness and strong separateness. These form the first threshold of capability beneath which to function as a human being is leading an impoverished life that will not be human at all.

Above the bare minimum level is the second threshold of higher capabilities. Here the person has to use one's own power of choice and self-definition, here one is capable of good functioning as a human being. The capabilities required for good functioning are called "Basic functional capabilities". They may be listed as:

- being able to live to the end of a human life of normal length,
- being able to have good health,
- being able to use the senses,
- being able to have attachment to things and persons outside ourselves,
- being able to form a conception of the good and to engage in critical reflection,
- being able to live for and with others,
- being able to live with concern for and in relation to animals, plans and the world of nature,
- being able to laugh, to play, to enjoy recreational activities,
- being able to live one's own life and nobody else's, and
- being able to live one's own life in one's own surroundings and context.

This section will discuss the application of basic functional capabilities to women, the gender through gender-aware policies and execution barriers to overcome through political, social and individual will and also the strategies to develop human capabilities.

One of the defining moments of the 20th century has been the relentless struggle for gender equality.. When this struggle finally succeeds—as it must—it will mark a great milestone in human progress. And along the way it will change most of today's premises for social, economic and political life. Let us hope that the success of that struggle will be one of the defining moments of the 21st century, because gender equality will enable both women and men to live lives of greater freedom and integrity. (UNDP, 2000)

Social Capital

It is true that poverty cannot be overcome without economic growth. The CCA strategy focuses on the household economy, the viability of which would get reflected in the national aggregate as well. And, as the strategy explains, the social capital generated by the coming together of people, even in a poor community, for a common purpose, would complement and energise the economic resources available and beyond the community.

There is a legitimate concern that, except in some cases where dedicated social activities and voluntary agencies have worked steadily for years, there exists not so much any "community spirit", as exploitation by whoever has power, and therefore conflict. The basic solvent for old problems of this nature is the opportunity of the poor to organize themselves, with the women's group in the forefront, their positive influence on the general assembly of the gram sabha, and the peaceful, patient pursuit of democratic procedure, consistent with the rule of law. There is no other known way to make representative institutions accountable to the electorate. (Enabling People's Intervention, Health Action, July 1998).

Amartya Sen while commenting about the accumulation of human capital and the expansion of human capability said that "If a person can become more productive in making commodities through better education, better health, and so on, it is not unnatural to expect that she can also directly achieve more—and have the freedom to achieve more—in leading her life. Both perspectives put humanity at the center of attention".

T.V. Rao points out that human resource development aims at ensuring that people in the country live longer; live happily, free of disease and hunger; have sufficient skill base to earn their own livelihood and well-being; have a sense of belongingness and pride through participation in determining their own destinies. The promotion of the well-being of individuals, families and societies provides a human resource agenda for all the countries the world over.

The Human Development Report, 2000 urges nations to commit themselves to gender equality in order to unleash the energy and productive capabilities of women around the world.

The Human Development Index measures the average achievements in a country in three basic dimensions of human development—a long and healthy life, knowledge and a decent standard of living. A composite index, the HDI thus contains three variables—life expectancy at birth, educational attainment (adult literacy and the combined gross primary, secondary and tertiary enrolment ratio) and GDP per capita (PPP US$). Income enters the HDI as a proxy for a decent standard of living and as a surrogate for all human choices not reflected in the other two dimensions.

HUMAN DEVELOPMENT INDEX

Same Dimensions, Different Indicators

Index	*Longevity*	*Knowledge*	*Decent standard of living*	*Participation of exclusion*
HDI	Life expectancy at birth	Adult literacy rate Combined enrolment ratio	Adjusted per capita income in PPP US$	—
GDI	Female and male life expectancy at birth	Female and male adult literacy rates Female and male combined enrol-ment ratios	Female and male per capita incomes (PPP US) based on females and male earned income shares	—
GEM	—	—	—	Economic & Political, Decision-making

UNDP Human Development Report.
HDI—Human Development Index
GDI—Gender-related Development Index
GEM—Gender Empowerment Measure

Development Indices to Selected Countries—HDI, GDI and GEM

S.No.	Countries	HDI	GDI	GEM
High Human Development				
1.	Norway	1	1	1
2.	Australia	2	2	9
3.	Canada	3	3	5
4.	Sweden	4	5	3
5.	Belgium	5	7	14
6.	United States	6	4	10
7.	Japan	9	11	31
8.	United Kingdom	14	12	16
9.	Denmark	15	13	12
10.	Austria	16	16	11
11.	Singapore	26	26	35
12.	Korea, Rep. of	27	29	61
13.	Kuwait	43	40	—
14.	United Arab Emirates	45	45	—
Medium Human Development				
15.	Mexico	51	49	37
16.	Malaysia	56	55	38
17.	Thailand	66	58	—
18.	Saudi Arabia	68	75	—
19.	Philippines	70	62	46
20.	Sri Lanka	81	70	56
21.	Turkey	82	71	63
22.	China	87	76	—
23.	South Africa	94	85	—
24.	Indonesia	102	92	—
25.	India	115	115	—
Low Human Development				
26.	Pakistan	127	117	—
27.	Nepal	129	120	—
28.	Bangladesh	132	121	62

Source: Human Development Report, 2001.

Human poverty among people towards illiteracy malnutrition highly the credited poor constructed like of gender mainstream activities. The government of India in economics mentioned that it is committed to the welfare of women through empowering them which is acknowledged from: "to adopt an integrated approach towards empowering women through effective convergence of existing services, financial and human resources, and infrastructure in both women-specific and women-related sectors".

Amartya Sen mentioned that the concept of human development draws on the magnificence of human potentiality amidst the widespread experience of narrowly circumscribed lives. Lack of schooling, meager health care, inadequate economic opportunities, violation of political liberties, denial of civil rights, and other hostile "winds" can totally frustrate human beings despite their potential to "ascend on the wings".

Mahbub ul Haq defines the Human Development as A Holistic Concept and says the human development paradigm covers all aspects of development—whether economic growth or international trade, budget deficits or fiscal policy, saving or investment or technology, basic social services or safety nets for the poor. No aspect of the development model falls outside its scope, but the vantage point is the widening of people's choices and the enrichment of their lives. All aspects of life—economic, political or cultural—are viewed from that perspective. Economic growth, as such, becomes only a subset of the human development paradigm.

On some aspects of the human development paradigm, there is fairly broad agreement:

- Development must put people at the centre of its concerns.
- The purpose of development is to enlarge all human choices, not just income.
- The human development paradigm is concerned both with building up human capabilities (through investment in people) and with using those human capabilities fully (through an enabling framework for growth and employment).
- Human development has four essential pillars: equality, sustainability, productivity and empowerment. It regards economic growth as essential but emphasizes the need to pay attention to its quality and distribution, analyses at length its link with human lives and questions its long-term sustainability.
- The human development paradigm defines the ends of development and analyses sensible option for achieving them.

Despite the broad agreement on many of these features, there are several controversies about the human development concept—often stemming from some misunderstanding about the concept itself. Fairly widespread is the mistaken view that human development is anti-growth and that it encompasses only social development.

The human development paradigm consistently takes the view that growth is not the end of economic development—but that the absence of growth often is. Economic growth is essential for human development, but no fully exploits the opportunities for improved well-being that growth offers, it needs to be properly managed. Some countries have been extremely successful in managing their economic growth to improve the human condition, others less so. So, there is no automatic link between economic growth and human progress. And one of the most pertinent policy issues concerns the exact process through which growth translates, or fails to translate, into human development under different development conditions.

There are four ways to create the desirable links between economic growth and human development.

First, emphasis on investment in the education, health and skills of the people can enable them to participate in the growth process as well as to share its benefits, principally through remunerative employment. This is the growth model adopted by China, Hong Kong, Japan, Malaysia, the Republic of Korea, Singapore, Thailand and many other newly industrializing countries.

Second, more equitable distribution of income and assets is critical for creating a close link between economic growth and human development. Wherever the distribution of income and assets is very uneven (as in Brazil, Nigeria and Pakistan), high GNP growth rates have failed to translate into people's lives. The link between distribution of assets and the nature of growth can be:

- Growth-led, with favourable initial conditions in asset distribution and mass education, including the participation of people in economic activities (China, the Republic of Korea).
- Unfavourable initial conditions but high growth with corrective public policy action, including people's participation (Chile, Malaysia).

- Low growth with public policy action to provide basic social services, but normally unsustainable over the long-term (Jamaica, Sri Lanka).

Third, some countries have managed to make significant improvement in human development even in the absence of good growth or good distribution. They have achieved this result through well-structured social expenditures by the government. Cuba, Jamaica, Sri Lanka and Zimbabwe, among others, achieved fairly impressive results through the generous state provision of social services. So did many countries is Eastern Europe and the Commonwealth of Independent States (CIS). But such experiments generally are not sustainable unless the economic base expands enough to support the social base.

Fourth, the empowerment of people—particularly women—is a sure way to link growth and human development. In fact, empowerment should accompany all aspects of life. If people can exercise their choices in the political, social and economic spheres, there is a good prospect that growth will be strong, democratic, participatory and durable (Mahbub ul Haq, 2005).

Selim Jahan while says about Evolution of the Human Development Index mentions that development is about enlarging people's choices by enhancing their functioning and capabilities. Development is of the people, for the people and by the people—"of the people" referring to human capital formation and human resources development through nutrition, health and education; "for the people" stressing the need for the benefits of economic growth to be translated into people's lives; and "by the people" meaning that people must be able to influence a process that affects their lives. Development must be shaped to fit people, as opposed to people being shaped to fit development (Selim Jahan, 2005)

WOMEN EMPOWERMENT, HUMAN RESOURCE DEVELOPMENT AND SUSTAINABLE DEVELOPMENT

The commonwealth heads of Government recognized that the Human Resource Development is the central to the promotion of sustainable development and reduction of poverty in the common-wealth countries. Human Resource Development involves women. It requires that the capabilities of women be improved, that disadvantages and discrimination be removed and that women have the opportunity to become active participants in all aspects of society through empowerment.

The process of empowerment involves not just an improvement in physical and social conditions but also equal participation in decision-making processes, control over resources and mechanisms for sustaining these gains.

The pioneer effort was enhanced through the Tamilnadu women Development under the assistance of the International find for Agricultural Development in eight districts of Tamilnadu in 1989. The prime objectives of the project were improve the social and economic position of women below poverty line, through the formation of self-help group of poor women in these districts with arise and supervision of NGOs, the main objectives of the project is the economic and social upliftment of women to enhance the welfare of their families and to improve their status in the family and community. The main objectives of the project are the economic and social upliftment of women to enhance he welfare of their families and to improve their status in the family and community. The objectives of economic upliftment under the project is sought to be achieved through increasing their incomes by integrating them into regular delivery system for credit and technical support services. On the other hand the social advancement is planned to be achieved by raising women's level of awareness and fostering the confidence to strive for social change through the development of strong and cohesive groups, which could be a source of mutual support for women.

While Sumi Krishna mentions about Community Development and Decentralisation in India, she summarized four different Indian approaches to the development of rural communities, from the 1950s to the present when explaining gender implications of approaches to rural development. Each of these approaches has been characterized by different interventional methods at the local level. The interventions have drawn upon, or themselves emerged from, particular response modes of the community and have required specific actions and behaviour from government and non-government interveners, including administrators, extension workers and development professionals. Participatory processes, self-help groups, micro-credit and micro-enterprises are currently being seen as the key means to empower poor Adivasi, Dalit and peasant women, and thereby to safeguard the sustainability of natural resources. These interventions have a rich prehistory in the Indian experience of community development, the mid-20th-century revival of traditional concepts of self-help such as the South Asian Shramdan and the Kenyan harambee (Thomas, 1980; Uphoff and Esman, 1974), and the customary role of rotating labour and credit associations in Asia, Africa and Latin America. Women were seen as being central to each of these earlier initiatives but usually as an undifferentiated homogenous category. Cutting across all approaches, women's self-help and micro-credit groups are now proliferating throughout India. Supported by government policy and NGO interventions, these are being seen as a magic wand for all the ills of development. The cognitive distance traversed between Shramdan, gift of labour, and today's Self-Help Groups encompasses half a century of development practice and different, overlapping approaches to community participation. (Sumi Krishna, 2004).

At present in participatory approach and the process has been emerged successful strategy in all-developmental programmes. Conventional approaches to community development and self-help are often paternalistic 'guided' methods of fostering participation. The search for alternatives to 'guided' participation can be traced to the Brazilian educator Paule Freire, who envisioned a process of conscientisation through which the oppressed would awaken to an awareness of the self, freeing individual creativity and knowledge, clearing the path towards an understanding of the structural roots of poverty and leading to collective actions. The encounter and communion between the people's worldview and the more 'sophisticated' view of the educators/leaders was the basis on which theory could be built. He argued that the 'true' praxis that makes dialogue possible involves action and reflection, not one or the other. Freire's revolutionary Pedagogy of the Oppressed (1970) inspired a range of participatory methodologies around the world and was a powerful impetus in South Asia as well. Participatory Action Research is one such method, widely used to raise individual and collective consciousness, and seen as transformative and libratory. It has now been overtaken by the Participatory Rural Appraisal approach. Even as the ideology of participation does not necessarily lead directly to political action, it does provide the scope for communities to develop their own knowledge, skills, understanding and energy, which are paths towards empowerment and resistance to subordination (Sumi Krishna, 2004).

Thus, women empowerment has impact on human resources development which leads to sustainable development.

Bibliography

Ahmad Jilani Syed Sadiq, 'Women in India—Legal and Human Rights', Centre for Professional Development in Higher Education and Women's Studies and Development Centre, New Delhi, 2004.

Argawal, Bina, 2010, "Gender and Green Governance: The Political Economy of Women's Presence Within and Beyond Community Forestry," New York, NY: Oxford University Press.

Bhasin, Kamla, "Understanding Gender", Kali for Women, New Delhi, 2000.

Bhuimali, Anil, "Poverty and Human Rights of Women", New Delhi: Serials Publications, 2005.

Burra, Neera, "Micro-credit, Poverty and Empowerment—Linking the Triad", New Delhi: Sage Publications India Pvt. Ltd., 2005.

Ciulla, Joanne B. (2004), "Leadership and the Problem of Bogus Empowerment", in Ciulla, Joanne B., *Ethics, the Heart of Leadership* (2nd ed.), Greenwood Publishing Group, ISBN 978-0-275-98248-5, "[...] in many organizations, promises of empowerment are bogus."

Dash, Dhanlaxmi, "Women, Environment and Health", Jaipur: Mangal Deep Publications, 2005.

Deolalikar, Anil B., "Attaining the Millennium Development Goals in India", New Delhi: Oxford University Press, 2005.

Desai, Neera and Usha Thakkar, 'Women in Indian Society', New Delhi: National Book Trust, 2004.

"Empowerment Takes More Than a Minute" by Ken Blanchard, John P. Carlos, and Alan Randolph.

Gupta, C.B. and N.P. Srinivasan, "Entrepreneurship Development in India", New Delhi: Sultan Cland & Sons, 2004.

International Encyclopedia of Women, Vol. 2, "Women Education and Empowerment," Dr. Digumarti Bhaskara Rao and Ms. Digumarti, Pushpa Latha (eds.), Discovery Publishing House, New Delhi, 1998.

Journal of Rural Development, NIRD, Hyderabad, Vol. 23(4), 2004, pp. 411-33.

Karmakar, K.G., "Rural Credit and Self-Help Groups, Micro-finance Needs and Concepts in India", New Delhi: Sage Publications India Pvt. Ltd., 2005.

Krishna Sumi, "Livelihood and Gender"—Equity in Community Resource Management, New Delhi: Sage Publications, 2004.

Krishnaraj Maithreyi, Remaking Society For Women-Visions: Past and Present, Indian Association of Women's Studies, 1995.

Kumar Dutta, Sujit and Dilip Kumar Ghosh, "Empowering Rural Women", New Delhi: Akorisha Publishing House, 2002.

Kumar Jha, Ashok, "Sustainable Development: Concept and Strategies", New Delhi: Adhyyan Publishers, 2004.

Mahalir Thittam-Working Manual, Tamil Nadu Corporation for Development of Women Ltd, Chennai.

Marilee, Karl, "Women and Empowerment Participation and Decision-making", London & New Jersey, Zed Books Ltd., 1995.

McGoldrick Jim, Stewart Jim and Watson Sandra, Understanding Human Resource Development—A Research-based Approach, Routledge, 2002.

Murthy, K. Ranjani, "Building Women's Capacities—Interventions in Gender Transformation", New Delhi, Sage Publications, 2001.

National Policy for the Empowerment of Women, 2001, Department of Women and Child Development, Ministry of Human Resource Development, Government of India.

Nussbaum C. Mortha, "Women and Human Development: The Capabiliteis Approach", New Delhi: Kali for Women, 2000.

Nussbaum, C. Martha, 1995, "Introduction," in Martha C. Nussbaum, and Jonathan Glover, eds. Women, Culture, and Development: A Study of Human Capabilities, pp. 1-15. Oxford: Clarendon Press.

Parr, Sakiko, Fukuda and A.K. Shiva Kumar, "Readings in Human Development", New York, Oxford University 2005.

Pieterse, Jan Nederveen, "Development Theory—Deconstruction/ Reconstructions", New Delhi: Vistaar Publications, 2001.

Potterfield, Thomas, "The Business of Employee Empowerment: Democracy and Ideaology in the Workplace," Quorum Books, 1999, p. 6.

Puthenkalam John Joseph, "Empowerment—Sustainable Human Development, Strategy for Poverty Alleviation", New Delhi: Rawat Publications, 2004.

Ramalaingam, G. and U. Jerinabi, "Women and Economic Development", Centre for Women's Studies, Avinashilingam Deemed University, Coimbatore, 2005.

Rao, T.V., "Human Resource Development: Experiences, Interventions, Strategies, New Delhi: Sage Publications Limited, 1996.

Rural Poverty Report, 2001, The Challenge of Ending Rural Poverty, New York: Oxford University Press, 2001.

Sahay, Sushama, "Women and Empowerment Approaches and Strategies", New Delhi; Discovery Publishing House, 1998.

Sahoo. R.K. and S.N. Tripathy, 'Self-Help Groups and Women Empowerment', New Delhi: Anmol Publications Pvt. Ltd., 2006.

Self-Help Group-Bank Linkage Programme, Fostering the Confidence of Empowerment among the Poorest of Women.

Self-Help Groups: Management, Department of Adult Education and Extension, Gandhigram University, 2000.

Sen, A.K. (1987): "Commodities and Capabilities", North-Holland, Amsterdam.

Sharma, Usha, "Gender Mainstreaming and Women's Rights", New Delhi: Authors Press, 2004.

Singha Roy, K. Debal, "Social Development and the Empowerment of Marginalized Groups—Perspectives and Strategies", New Delhi: Sage Publications, 2003.

Stewart, Aileen Mitchell, *Empowering People* (Institute of Management), Pitman, London: Financial Times Management, 1994.

Sughosh India Foundation, "Sughosh's Meaning of Empowerment", 8 Nov. 2010 (accessed October 4, 2011).

Tamil Nadu Women's Development Project—Terminal Evaluation Report; Agricultural Finance Corporation Ltd., Chennai, 1999.

Thilagavathi, G. and B. Regina Papa, "Gender Sensitization—Course Material", published by Tamil Nadu Police Department, 2003.

Thomas, K.W. and Velthouse, B.A. (1990), "Cognitive Elements of Empowerment: An 'Interpretive' Model of Intrinsic Task Motivation", *Academy of Management Review*, Vol. 15, No. 4, 666-81.

UNDP (1993), The Human Development Report, Oxford University Press, Delhi

UNICEF, 2007, "Equality in Employment," in The State of the World's Children, New York: United Nations Children's Fund.

United Nations Research Institute for Social Development, 2010, Combating Poverty and Inequality: Structural Change, Social Policy and Politics, Geneva: UNRISD "Gender Inequalities at Home and in the Market," Chapter 4, pp. 5-33.

Vanessa Griffen, Women, Development and Empowerment: A Pacific Feminist Perspective, Asian and Pacific Development Centre, Kuala Lumpur, 1987.

"Welcome to Micro-Empowering!", Micro-empowering.org. Retrieved 2012-08-24.

Wilkinson, A., 1998, Empowerment: Theory and Practice, *Personnel Review* [online], Vol. 27, No. 1, 40-56. Accessed February 16, 2004.

World Survey on the Role of Women in Development, 2009, Women's Control over Economic Resources and Access to Financial Resources, including Microfinance, New York: United Nations.

Index